# American Heritage 1500–1900

P. J. LARKIN, M.Sc., B.A.

*Illustrated by Dorothy H. Ralphs*

HULTON EDUCATIONAL PUBLICATIONS

ISBN 0 7175 0783 1

*First published 1977 by*
HULTON EDUCATIONAL PUBLICATIONS LIMITED
*Raans Road, Amersham, Bucks.*

*Printed in Great Britain by*
*The Camelot Press Ltd, Southampton*

# Contents

# Spanish Gold

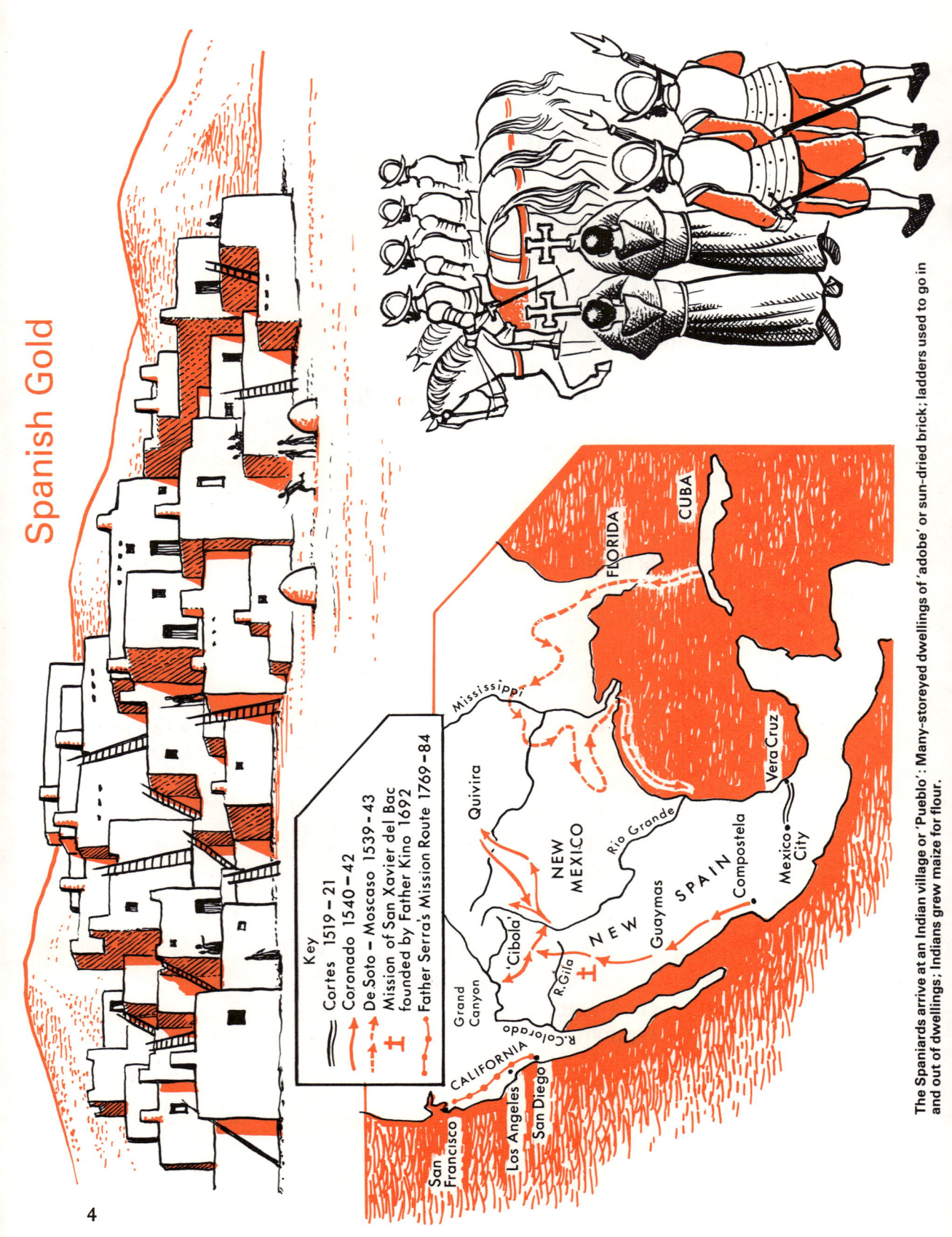

Key
 — Cortes 1519 – 21
→ Coronado 1540 – 42
⇢ De Soto – Moscaso 1539 – 43
✝ Mission of San Xavier del Bac
   founded by Father Kino 1692
✝ Father Serra's Mission Route 1769 – 84

FLORIDA

CUBA

Mississippi

VERA CRUZ

Quivira

NEW MEXICO

Rio Grande

NEW SPAIN

Compostela

Mexico City

Guaymas

'Cibola'

R. Gila

Grand Canyon

R. Colorado

CALIFORNIA

Los Angeles

San Diego

San Francisco

**The Spaniards arrive at an Indian village or 'Pueblo': Many-storeyed dwellings of 'adobe' or sun-dried brick; ladders used to go in and out of dwellings; Indians grew maize for flour.**

4

# Spanish Gold

After Columbus had discovered the New World in his voyages to the West Indies (1492–3) the Spaniards, under their famous soldier-explorers Cortes and Pisarro, began to settle in South America and to conquer two great American civilisations, the Aztecs in Mexico and the Incas of Peru. In Mexico the Spaniards found gold.

So eager were the Spaniards to take back gold to their own country that they believed huge quantities of it lay also to the north. Stories they had heard, sometimes incredible and fantastic, of the wealth and wonder of the unknown lands to the north, encouraged soldiers like Ponce de Leon to set sail on voyages of discovery. It was on Easter Sunday in 1513 that Ponce first saw the coast of Florida, so named because the Spaniards call Easter Sunday 'Pascua Florida' (flowery Easter).

Another famous Spanish explorer was De Soto who, in 1539, landed at Tampa Bay in Florida and during the next three years explored areas now known as Florida, Georgia, North and South Carolina, Tennessee, Alabama, Arkansas and Texas. He and his men were the first Europeans to see the Mississippi.

One of the strangest of Spanish stories linked together Estevan, a negro slave, Marcos, a Franciscan friar and Francesco Coronado, a noble and officer in the Spanish army. Their travels brought them to the river Colorado and the desert of Lower California. The friar and the negro went north in 1539 to find 'Cibola', the 'Seven Cities of Gold'. Estevan was killed, but Marcos brought back a tale of a city whose temple walls were studded with precious stones and whose people wore girdles of gold.

In February, 1540 Coronado set out from Compostela in Mexico to find the reported treasure. He was accompanied by Spanish horsemen and foot-soldiers, a thousand friendly Indians, cattle for food, priests for prayers and the friar. Coronado travelled north for over a thousand miles, making his way through deserts, over mountain passes and into the country of the wild Apaches, only to find that the 'Seven Golden Cities' were nothing but primitive Indian villages, whose mud huts had glittered in the Arizona sun to fire the friar's imagination.

Marcos was sent home in disgrace but Coronado now went east, searching for another town of gold 'where the lord of that country took his afternoon nap under a great tree hung with bells of gold'. When they reached 'Quivira' they found only the straw-hutted villages of the Wichita Indians and a copper necklace worn by an Indian chief. They returned sad, weary and shame-faced to Mexico City, but they were the first Europeans to see the Grand Canyon, the buffalo, the wide treeless plains and the villages of the Pueblo Indians.

## Things to do

A. Answer these questions:
1 Which parts of America did (a) Cortes (b) Pisarro conquer?
2 How did Florida get its name?
3 What parts of America did De Soto explore?
4 What were the Spaniards always searching for?
5 What did the 'Seven Golden Cities' turn out to be?
6 What did the Spaniards find at 'Quivira'?

B. Make a copy of the map and picture and tell its story.

C. Write about: Cortes, Pisarro, Ponce de Leon, De Soto.

D. Tell the story of Coronado's search for gold.

# Spanish Priests and Missions

A Spanish mission in California in the eighteenth century

# Spanish Priests and Missions

Besides winning gold, the Spaniards also wanted to win the hearts of the native Indians for the cause of Christianity. One of the most famous explorer-priests was Father Kino, who had been sent by his Jesuit Superiors in 1687 to live among the Pima Indians of North West Mexico. He spent the next twenty-one years of his life exploring the dry, broken mountain passes and the fertile, irrigated valleys until he had mapped and visited every part of this country. Sometimes accompanied by other Jesuit priests, but often with only his personal servant and an Indian guide, he rode out into the sun to travel up to six hundred miles (960 km) on any one expedition.

He insisted that California was not an island, but a peninsula joined to the mainland. From a vantage-point on the hill of Santa Clara he was able to show a visiting priest the truth of his belief. Father Kino was one of the true founders of the American West and you can still see today, near the aerodrome in Tucson, Arizona, the mission of San Xavier del Bac which he set up in 1692. Other priests established missions throughout Lower and Upper California for many years until the beginning of the nineteenth century.

The exploration and settlement of Upper California was carried on by Captain Gaspar de Portola (1769–70), who worked his way along the land route from San Diego to San Francisco Bay. Wherever the Captain built a fort, Father Serra, a Franciscan priest, built a mission to teach and convert the Indians. From San Diego to San Francisco he tramped along in the hot sun through scrubland and desert, stopping on saints' days to ring his bell and cry, 'Come and receive the faith of Christ'. His route is still marked by the flowers of the mustard plant whose seed he scattered as he walked. By the time of his death in 1784, Upper California had been successfully colonised around its missions, one of which, built in 1776, still stands in San Francisco today.

The defeat of the Spanish Armada in 1588 cost Spain the control of the Atlantic Ocean which passed to the English and French. Her empire on the west coast of America tended to become more and more remote, until it was taken over by the Mexicans in 1821. After the war of 1848 between the U.S.A. and Mexico, the earlier Spanish colonies became the American states of California, Nevada, Arizona and Texas. Florida was sold to the U.S.A. by Spain in 1819.

But the Spaniards had left their mark. From them the Americans had learned the life of ranching and rodeos. 'Cowboy' is a translation of the Spanish word 'vaquero' and other words connected with cowboys, such as 'corral', 'mustang', 'patio', 'sombrero', 'desperado' and 'bronco', are all of Spanish origin. The Spaniards' strong religious beliefs also left traces in America and names like Los Angeles (The Angels) and San Francisco (St. Francis) remain today, to remind us of those sturdy figures in their black or brown habits who strode out into the sun.

## Things to do

A. Answer these questions:
   1 Where was Father Kino sent? When?
   2 What did he prove about California?
   3 What was Father Serra's route?
   4 What did he build?
   5 What happened to the Spanish settlements in 1821 and 1848?
   6 What did Spain give to America?

B. Make a copy of the picture and write about it.

C. Tell the story of Father Kino and Father Serra.

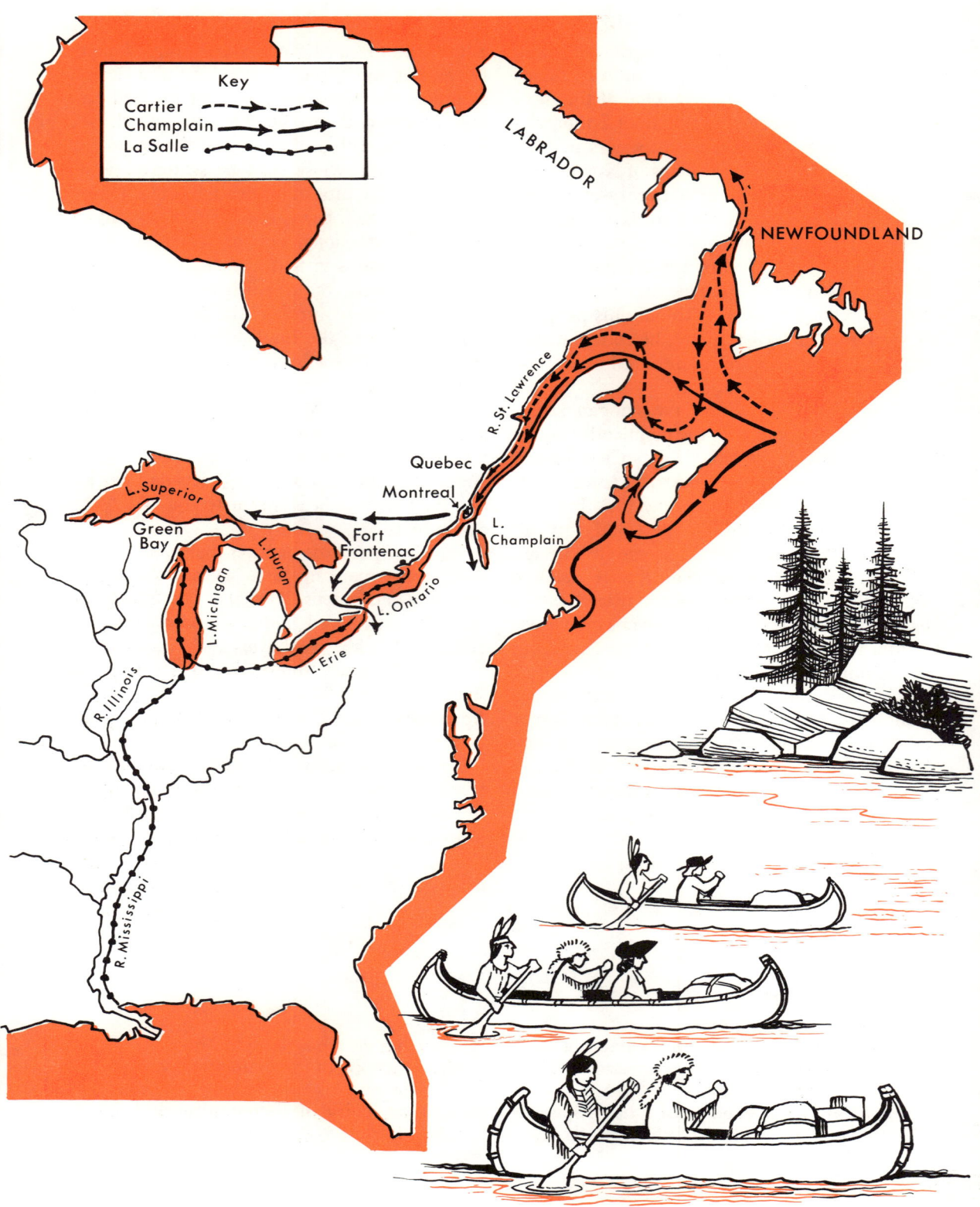

Key
Cartier
Champlain
La Salle

LABRADOR

NEWFOUNDLAND

R. St. Lawrence

Quebec
Montreal

L. Champlain

L. Superior

Green Bay

L. Michigan

L. Huron

Fort Frontenac

L. Ontario

L. Erie

R. Illinois

R. Mississippi

# The French in North America (1)

While the Spanish pushed their way into North America from a land base, the French made their entry from the sea. Following the voyages of Cabot (1497–98), French fishermen began fishing the waters of Newfoundland and so started the exploration of the great estuary of the St. Lawrence which led into the interior of Canada. By 1535 Jacques Cartier, merchant and navigator of St. Malo, had moved up the river and penetrated as far as Montreal.

But no settlement was made by the French until Champlain sailed up the St. Lawrence and explored the area around the Great Lakes. Champlain was a soldier, sailor and geographer who had been sent out to develop the fur trade and to look for the inland sea which would lead to the East. Champlain is remembered as the founder of Quebec and as the first governor of French Canada.

In spite of Champlain's efforts, New France (as Canada became known) contained only a handful of traders, missionaries and officials by the middle of the seventeenth century. The recognition of New France as a royal province in 1663 and the arrival of La Salle, began a new era of settlement.

La Salle was the son of a wealthy merchant of Rouen. He first thought of becoming a priest, but at the age of twenty-two he decided to join his brother near Montreal. It was a dangerous area, liable to attack by the Indians. The priests of the St. Sulpice Mission were glad to grant land to a vigorous newcomer who could defend and develop it. About eight miles outside Montreal, La Salle built a village and palisade. He rented out land to his tenants for three chickens each a year and developed his own personal estate. He grew wheat and raised cattle and sheep.

La Salle spoke to the Indians who landed their furs near his estate. He learned their language and listened to their talk about the 'Missi-sipi', the 'Mighty River'. He wondered whether it would lead to China. He named his farm 'La Chine' (China), perhaps as a joke, perhaps because he really meant it; for the Mississippi was to dominate his whole life, either as the elusive pathway to the East or as a real commercial waterway from the St. Lawrence to the Gulf of Mexico.

In the summer of 1669 he sold his lands, bought supplies and hired men and canoes to go in search of the Mississippi. The small band started off from the waters of Lake St. Louis and made their way via Lake Ontario, Tina-watawa, Onondoga and the head waters of the river Ohio. His men would go no further and he was left to make his own way back to Montreal in the spring of 1670.

The Count of Frontenac became governor of New France in 1672 and La Salle found a new friend and ally. Together they built Fort Frontenac and made it an important centre of the fur trade. La Salle prospered. He built a village and estate around the fort and was granted the rank of nobleman, following a visit to France.

In 1677 he was restless again, haunted by the vision of the Mississippi carrying his ships and his cargoes to the Gulf of Mexico and so to Europe. He went to France to get support from King Louis XIV and returned in 1678 with new authority to build ships and forts along his route from Lake Ontario to the Mississippi.

## Things to do

A. Answer these questions:
  1 What did Cartier explore?
  2 What area did Champlain explore?
  3 Where did La Salle join his brother?
  4 Why was the Mississippi so important for him?
  5 What did La Salle do in 1669?
  6 What did he do in 1677–8?

B. Make a neat copy of the map and tell the story of the picture.

C. Write about: Cartier, Champlain, Montreal, the Mississippi, Fort Frontenac.

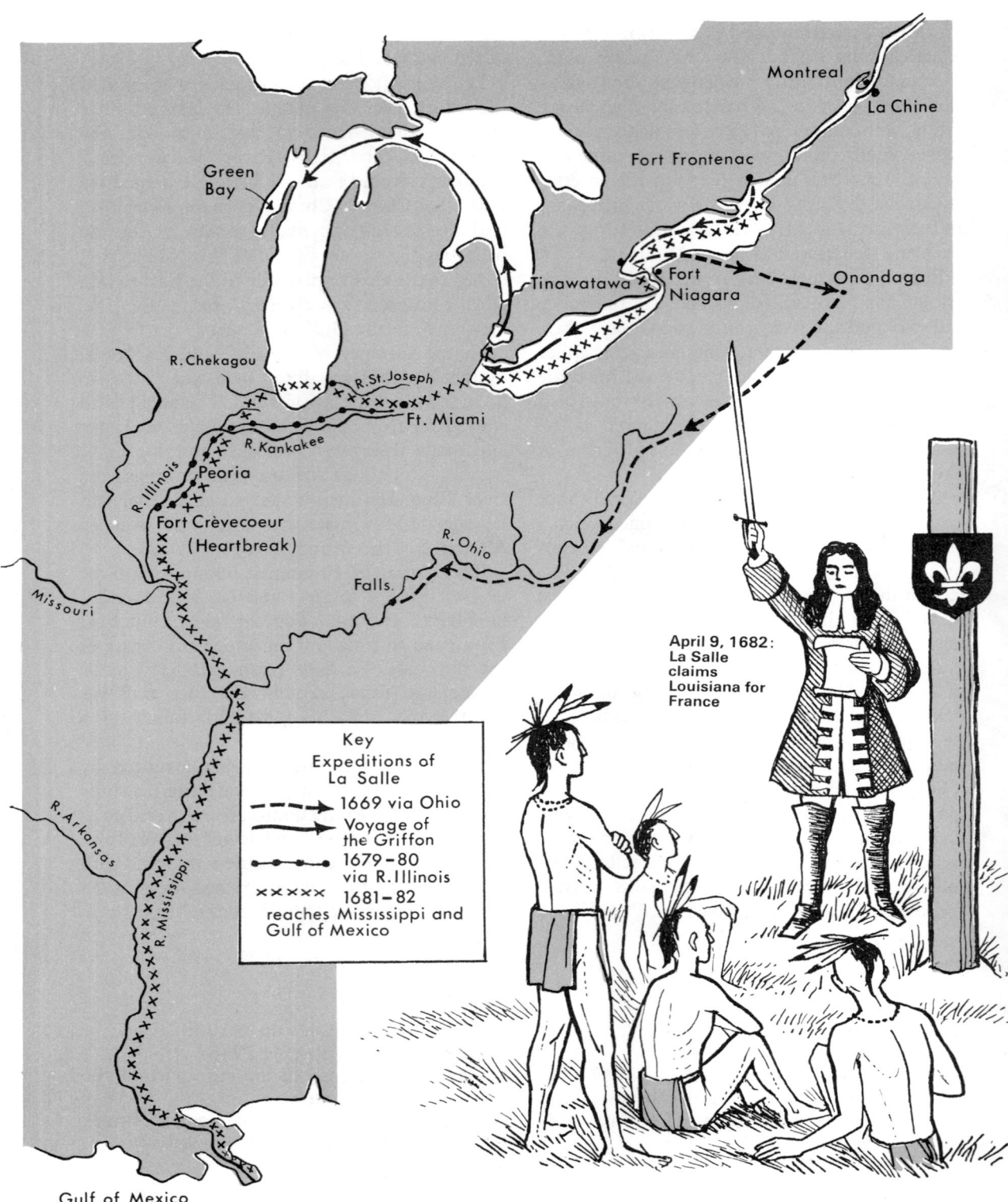

Montreal

La Chine

Fort Frontenac

Green Bay

Tinawatawa

Fort Niagara

Onondaga

R. Chekagou

R. St. Joseph

Ft. Miami

R. Kankakee

Peoria

R. Illinois

Fort Crèvecoeur
(Heartbreak)

R. Ohio

Falls.

Missouri

R. Arkansas

R. Mississippi

Gulf of Mexico

April 9, 1682:
La Salle
claims
Louisiana for
France

**Key**
**Expeditions of**
**La Salle**

———➤ 1669 via Ohio
———➤ Voyage of
the Griffon
•—•—•—• 1679–80
via R. Illinois
×××××× 1681–82
reaches Mississippi and
Gulf of Mexico

# The French in North America (2)

By the summer of 1679 La Salle had built Fort Niagara and launched a forty-five ton ship, the *Griffon* on Lake Erie. He sailed to Green Bay in his new ship and then disembarked with his men for another Mississippi expedition. The *Griffon* set out for Fort Niagara with a cargo of furs but was never heard of again.

La Salle, unaware of the loss of the *Griffon*, pressed on with his plan to reach the Mississippi. This time he and his men tried a different route. They started off from Green Bay and paddled down the waters of Lake Michigan through storms that soaked them all to the skin. Game was scarce and they lived on wild berries and the carcass of a deer, from which they drove a flock of scavenging birds. They reached the end of the lake and came to the St. Joseph river. They built Fort Miami and then pushed on to the Kankakee. They linked up with the river Illinois and travelled on as far as Peoria. Here La Salle built another fort which he called 'Fort Heartbreak', for news of the loss of the *Griffon* had filtered through and most of his men had left him again. He laid the keel of another ship and then made the awesome journey all the way back to the palisade and blockhouses of Fort Frontenac. At the end of a thousand miles (1600 km) and sixty-seven days of swamp and forest, soaked by day and frozen by night, he reached home on May 6, 1680.

Everything was wrong. Cargoes had been lost on the Great Lakes and on the St. Lawrence. His property had been seized because of debts, and when he went back to the Illinois river in August, 1680 he found Fort Heartbreak destroyed, the half-finished ship abandoned and the site deserted.

La Salle would not give up. He set out in the autumn of 1681 from Lake Ontario with thirty men. He reached Fort Miami in November. They were off again in December in the grip of Canada's icy winter. They dragged their canoes on sledges across the frozen waters of Lake Michigan to reach the Chekagou river and then made their way to the river Illinois and on to Peoria. Here they found open water and the first signs of spring, snow melting and the appearance of birds and animals. They paddled their birch-bark canoes down the river to join the Mississippi on February 6, 1682.

They passed the mouth of the Missouri with its rushing, muddy waters and saw the Ohio on their left a few days later. They entered the country of the Arkansas Indians and hunted for fresh food. By the middle of March they came to the mouth of the Arkansas river. This was the farthest point reached by earlier French explorers. They continued south and came to warm sunshine, flowering peach trees and vines everywhere. They exchanged gifts with the Tensa Indians who worshipped the sun, and finally tasting the salty tang and feeling the fresh breeze of the open sea, they paddled out on to the silent, deserted and vast expanse of the Gulf of Mexico (April, 1682).

This was La Salle's moment of triumph. The little band gathered together. While the priests led the singing of psalms and the men called out, 'Vive le Roi' (Long live the King), La Salle claimed the lands of the Mississippi for France and named them 'Louisiana', after his king.

In 1684 he left France with four ships, to return to the Mississippi. The expedition failed to find the mouth of the river and La Salle was killed while trying to find it by moving across land (1687).

## Things to do

A.  Answer these questions:
  1  Name three forts built by La Salle.
  2  Why was 1680 a bad year for him?
  3  When did he reach the Gulf of Mexico?
  4  What land did he claim for France?

B.  Make a copy of the map and tell the story of the picture.
C.  Describe La Salle's journey down the Mississippi.
D.  Write your own story of the life of La Salle.

Jamestown—
Virginia 1607

12

# Jamestown—Virginia 1607

After Drake returned from the Pacific Ocean and Spanish America in 1580 with a ship crammed with gleaming, golden treasure, it was easy to persuade the English, like the French and Spaniards before them, that America was the land where quick and easy fortunes could be made. Every sailor in port told the same story of a land where 'they gather rubies and diamonds by the shore to hang on their children's coats and stick to their caps'. Rich merchants saw a chance of solid investment in virgin lands. They pooled their wealth by joining together in trading companies backed by a royal charter and the authority of the crown.

Sir Walter Raleigh tried to make a settlement on Roanoke Island, which he called Virginia in honour of Queen Elizabeth, but the perils and hardships of emigrant life were too much for the settlers. Some twenty years later a charter was granted to the London and Plymouth trading companies, to try again, along the American coast between the 34th and 45th parallels. The three ships sent by the London Company reached Chesapeake Bay and sailed up the James river to a wooded island which they called Jamestown (1607).

The new settlement was surrounded by an unhealthy swamp and overlooked by dense forest. The colonists had no idea how to live in their strange new world. They ate up their supplies in seven months. They quarrelled. They stole. Some died. After two years there were only thirty-eight left out of the original one hundred and five who had landed. They packed up, ready to go home, but the settle-ment was saved by an incoming ship which brought new supplies and people.

They found a leader in Captain John Smith who forced everyone to work on pain of being thrown out beyond the stockade, to face starvation or death from hostile Indians. 'He that will not work neither shall he eat!' The settlers tried growing crops, but the burning summers produced more mosquitoes than corn. Then a plant grown by the Indians was discovered by the settlers to be as valuable as gold. The future of Virginia was assured when the first shipment of tobacco left for England. Cured in smoke-houses and graded by hand, Virginian tobacco was soon able to compete with the best Spanish tobacco smoked in England.

The colony prospered. Better colonists, small landowners and hard-working labourers, came over from England. The Virginians moved out of the stockade and built houses of brick, a hospital and a church. In July, 1619 twenty-two men selected by the governor met in Jamestown church to help with the government of the colony. This was where American democracy began.

Virginia was the first of the English settlements on the east coast of North America. Eventually they grew into thirteen colonies. The plantation colonies in the South—which included Virginia (1607), Maryland (1634), North and South Carolina (1663) and Georgia (1733)—sent their tobacco, rice, indigo and cotton down the rivers and across the seas to England, the West Indies and to many parts of America.

## Things to do

A. Answer these questions:
   1 What did the English hope to find in America?
   2 Who first tried to colonise Virginia?
   3 Which companies were granted a charter?
   4 Which part of America did it cover?
   5 Where did the colonists land?
   6 What problems did they face?
   7 What saved them?
   8 Name four plantation colonies.

B. Make a copy of the picture and tell the story of the early settlers.

C. Write about: Captain John Smith, Sir Walter Raleigh, tobacco.

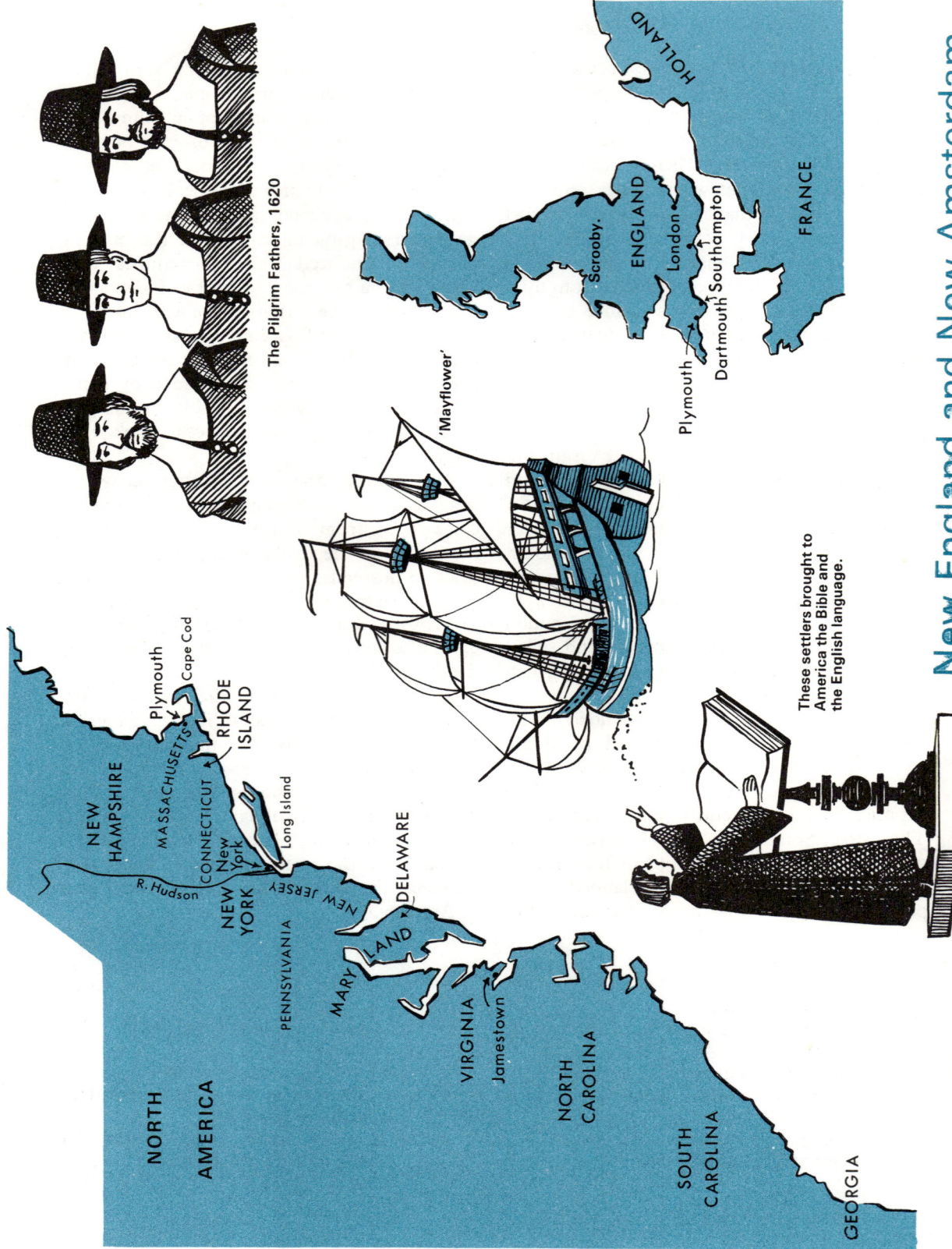

New England and New Amsterdam

The Pilgrim Fathers, 1620

HOLLAND

ENGLAND

Scrooby.

London

Dartmouth Southampton

Plymouth

FRANCE

'Mayflower'

These settlers brought to America the Bible and the English language.

NORTH AMERICA

Plymouth
Cape Cod
RHODE ISLAND

NEW HAMPSHIRE

MASSACHUSETTS

CONNECTICUT

Long Island

New York

R. Hudson

NEW YORK

NEW JERSEY

DELAWARE

PENNSYLVANIA

MARYLAND

VIRGINIA

Jamestown

NORTH CAROLINA

SOUTH CAROLINA

GEORGIA

# New England and New Amsterdam

In the year 1608 a group of Puritans, from the village of Scrooby in Lincolnshire, decided to leave England and go to Holland where they could follow their religion in peace and be free from the harsh laws of King James I (1603–25) of England.

In Holland, however, they missed English things and English ways. Hearing of English settlements in North America, they resolved to find peace and freedom of worship in this new land overseas.

They put their money into two ships, the *Mayflower* and the *Speedwell*, but the latter proved leaky as a sieve. After stops at Southampton, Dartmouth and Plymouth, the remaining settlers crowded into the *Mayflower* and set out for America on September 6, 1620. This was the historic voyage of the Pilgrim Fathers.

It was a small ship. With one hundred and two passengers, as well as crew, there was only enough space for each one to spread his mattress. They were tossed about by severe storms and drenched by the water which poured through the leaky decks. It was always cold. It took sixty-six days to cross the Atlantic, but only one passenger died and one woman gave birth to a son, who was given the apt—though strange—name 'Oceanus' (The Ocean).

On November 9 they sighted land and two days later the *Mayflower* was anchored off Cape Cod in Provincetown harbour. Exploratory parties were sent out to find the best place for a settlement. They chose the site of Plymouth (named after the English town) because the land had been cleared by the Indians and there was a useful harbour and a plentiful supply of water. They built a community house and nineteen smaller houses for the settlers. On January 21, 1621 they held their first service ashore.

While the English were building up their settlements at Jamestown and Plymouth, the Dutch were laying the foundations of the modern city of New York, which they called New Amsterdam. It was an Englishman, Henry Hudson, employed by the Dutch, who sailed into New York Bay and up the Hudson river in 1609, to claim the area for Holland.

In 1623 the Dutch sent over thirty families to form the colony of New Amsterdam on Manhattan Island and three years later they bought the island from the Indians for presents worth twenty dollars. They built a fort and a wall to protect their colony. Battery Point still stands on the site of the fort and Wall Street marks the line of the old wall. The part of New York known as the 'Bowery' was originally the Dutch governor's garden.

The Dutch colony spread north from New Amsterdam up the Hudson and included a part of Long Island and Connecticut. It was known as the Dutch province of New Netherlands. Like the Spaniards, the French and the English, the Dutch left their mark on America. They gave New York its international character and famous Dutch families such as the Stuyvesants, Van Burens, Schylers, Vanderbilts, Rockefellers and Roosevelts, continued to guide the fortunes of the U.S.A. well into the twentieth century.

The English in New England always regarded the Dutch in New Amsterdam as interlopers. In 1664 a British force under James, Duke of York, brother of King Charles II, took over the city of New Amsterdam and the province of New Netherlands. The Dutch city was re-named New York and the former Dutch territory became part of two new English colonies, New York and New Jersey.

The English built up thirteen colonies on the east coast of North America. There were five plantation colonies in the south, four New England settlements in the north, Massachusetts (including Plymouth and Maine), New Hampshire, Rhode Island and Connecticut, and four middle colonies, New York, New Jersey, Pennsylvania and Delaware.

## Things to do

A.  Answer these questions:
1  Why did the Puritans sail to America?
2  Where did they land?
3  Name their settlement.
4  What colony did the Dutch build up?

5  List the names of the English colonies.
B.  Make a neat copy of the diagram.
C.  Tell the story of the Pilgrim Fathers.
D.  Write about the Dutch in America.

# The Indians of the High Plains

The Buffalo Hunt

# The Indians of the High Plains

The High Plains run down the middle of the North American continent from Saskatchewan and Alberta in Canada to the deserts of New Mexico. They are bounded on the west by the Rocky mountains, on the east by the Great Lakes and the Missouri and Mississippi rivers. They consisted originally of a huge expanse of grassland, largely flat, treeless, bitterly cold in winter and burning hot in summer. This was the home of the nomadic Plains Indians: the Sioux, Cheyenne, Comanche, Arapaho, Kiowa, Assiniboin, Crow, Blackfoot and Apache.

The horse and the buffalo played a vital part in the life of the Indian. Big strong horses were used to drag the 'travois', a frame made up on two tepee poles attached to the sides of the animal and pulled like a sledge along the ground. When the tribe was on the move it would be used to carry family goods and personal possessions, as well as very young children and the old and infirm.

A smaller, lighter mount was used for hunting or war. This horse had to be courageous and well-trained, able to wait without a sound, ready to come at call or whistle, fearless in face of arrow, gun or spear. When the Indian died he was sometimes wrapped in a shroud and placed on an eight-foot (2·4 m) scaffold away from wild animals. Something taken from his favourite horse would be tied on to the pole of the scaffold, so that he could go on riding, defiant and free, in the new world beyond the sun. The Comanche were the finest horsemen of the plains.

The great event of the year was the summer buffalo hunt, when the tribes came together after the harsh, lean months of the winter. The most detailed preparations were made for the hunt. Horses would be carefully chosen and decorated with fine feathers. The men would pick out their best bows, made from green wood bent into shape and strengthened with strips of buffalo sinew, stuck on with glue. Sometimes they would pursue the roaming buffaloes for vast distances, taking food, clothes and tepee packed on the travois. They would live on pemmican, a strong-smelling but nourishing mixture of dried meat, berries, bone marrow and melted fat, packed in strips.

The buffalo was not only a basic food for the Indian; it also provided him with blankets, moccasins, mittens, shirts and leggings. Sinew was turned into thread or bowstring, bones into tools, horns into cups, ladles and spoons. The buffalo's stomach became a water bottle, the rough side of its tongue a hairbrush, its oily fat a dressing for the hair and its hide a covering for the tepee. He traded some of his buffalo meat and hides for corn, vegetables and other agricultural produce, from the farming tribes who lived on the edge of the plains.

The plains' Indian kept on the move, so his home was a light, portable tepee, made from six or more buffalo hides stretched over poles like a skin to make the shape of a cone. At the top there was a smoke hole and two flaps which could be adjusted to prevent the smoke from blowing back in and to ensure a good draught for the fire. During the harsh winter months when food was scarce, the tribe split into small groups or families, each to fend for itself. They would pitch their tepee in any available shelter, behind a rock, bank or small hill, and pass the long, dark evenings around the fire, telling stories of great chiefs, of good and bad spirits, of feast and famine, of the triumphs and tragedies which went to make up the history of their tribe.

## Things to do

A. Answer these questions:
   1 Where did the High Plains lie?
   2 Name five Indian tribes.
   3 Name the great event of the Indian year.
   4 Name two animals vital to the Indian.
   5 What did the buffalo provide for the Indian?
   6 Explain the words: travois, pemmican, tepee.
B. Make a copy of the picture and tell its story.
C. Describe a buffalo hunt.
D. Write about the life of the Indian.

# America Quarrels with Britain 1765–1775

British defeat the French and remove the French danger from the American colonists.

British government told the colonists they must provide men or money to defend their country.

The colonists refused to provide men or money, so the British government taxed them.

The Boston Massacre 1770
Trouble breaks out in Boston.

The Boston Tea Party
Trouble in Boston again

Philadelphia—first American 'Rebel' Congress

Fighting starts in Lexington.

On July 4, 1776 the Americans made their famous Declaration of Independence.

# America Quarrels with Britain 1765–1775

England had provided the goods, the people and the ships to set up the English colonies on the east coast of North America. The colonists were still the subjects of the King of England in their new world and had to obey his laws. The English parliament controlled the trade between England and North America and the colonists were expected to deal only with the mother country, exchanging their raw materials for English manufactured goods. Colonial industries were discouraged.

As long as the colonists needed the British army to defend them against the French and the Indians, they put up with the trade regulations—which were not always strictly enforced. The situation changed between 1756 and 1763 when the British defeated the French and took over their lands in North America.

The government in London felt that the colonists should pay something towards the cost of keeping British troops in North America. In 1765 the English parliament passed the Stamp Act which introduced a new tax, payable by attaching special stamps to legal papers and documents. The colonists refused to buy the stamps and the Act was cancelled. But the British government insisted on its right to tax the colonists and put duties on a small number of goods imported into America, including glass, paper and tea.

The Americans protested angrily that the British government had no right to tax them without their consent and they refused to buy the goods on which duties had been placed.

Opposition to the British parliament spread from New England in the North to Virginia in the South, but many loyal Americans still hoped that the quarrel with the British might be settled in a friendly way. Violent events in Boston made this impossible and turned what had started as a protest into open rebellion and finally war.

In 1770 a British sentry in Boston was attacked by a mob and in the riot that followed four local people were killed. This event was condemned throughout the colonies as the 'Boston Massacre'. In 1773 some ships of the British East India Company, loaded with tea, tied up in Boston harbour. The tax on tea was very unpopular and young men from Boston boarded the ships and threw the chests of tea, worth eighteen thousand pounds in all, into the sea.

Angered by the 'Boston Tea Party', the British government closed the port of Boston and put British troops under General Gage in the town to keep law and order. The colonists now openly rebelled against the British and began to call up volunteers to form a rebel army. In April, 1775 British troops were fired on by Americans at Concord and Lexington, not far from Boston. Rebel forces next occupied Bunker Hill, which overlooked General Gage's headquarters in Boston. British troops drove the Americans from the hill, but suffered heavy losses, and the Battle of Bunker Hill, June 17, 1775 marked the beginning of the War of American Independence.

## Things to do

A. Answer these questions:
 1 What event changed the situation between 1756 and 1763?
 2 What did England want the colonists to do?
 3 What act was passed in 1765?
 4 What did the Americans refuse to do?
 5 What events in Boston made the quarrel worse?
 6 What event marked the beginning of the War of Independence?
B. Make a neat copy of the diagram.
C. Write about: Stamp Act, Boston Massacre, Boston Tea Party, Bunker Hill.

George Washington and the War of
American Independence

# George Washington and the War of American Independence

George Washington was born in Virginia in 1732. He joined the Virginian army in 1752 and fought on the western frontier against the French. He left the army in 1758 with the rank of Brigadier-General and settled down on the family estate at Mount Vernon. He supported the colonists in their struggle against the British government and in May, 1775 he was made Commander-in-Chief of the American forces, a post he held throughout the War of American Independence from 1775 to 1783.

In the spring of 1776 Washington forced the British to leave Boston and to abandon two hundred cannon and invaluable stores, but he was badly defeated on Brooklyn heights on Long Island, losing five thousand men. Under cover of fog he managed to ferry the remainder of his troops across to Manhattan, only to be pushed back again from White Plains across the Hudson and towards the Delaware. The situation was very bad for the Americans. On Christmas night 1776, however, Washington marched on Trenton and defeated the German troops attached to the British, capturing many prisoners and a large quantity of arms and ammunition. General Cornwallis chased after him with a much larger British force, but Washington gave him the slip during the night and went on to defeat three British regiments at Princeton.

This success encouraged the colonists and recruits came flocking in during the spring of 1777, though there was more trouble ahead. Washington was driven back again at Brandywine Creek in September and the British captured Philadelphia, forcing the rebel government to rush off into the interior of Pennsylvania. The American commander retreated to Valley Forge where he had to sit out a brutal winter. 'The winds whistled, the food gave out, the fields stank with death and disease.' He held on until the spring, though he lost half his men.

Elsewhere the news was better for the Americans. British forces under General Burgoyne suffered a heavy defeat at Saratoga in October, 1777 and in the summer of 1778 the French came into the war on the side of the Americans.

The second part of the war was fought in the South. After early successes in South Carolina and Georgia, British forces under General Cornwallis retired to Yorktown in Virginia in 1781. American forces under George Washington, supported by French troops on land and by a French fleet in the harbour, forced Cornwallis to surrender on October 19, 1781. This was the last important battle of the war, which ended with the Treaty of Paris in 1783. Britain recognised the full independence of the American colonies.

In December, 1783 Washington gave up his military command and returned to Mount Vernon. He was called to Philadelphia in 1787 to act as chairman of the Federal Convention, whose task was to work out a constitution for the new nation. In April, 1789 he became the first President of the U.S.A. and held this post until 1796. He helped to rebuild the U.S.A. after eight years of war and gave her a strong government and a respected place among the nations of the world.

## Things to do

A. Answer these questions:
1 To what post was Washington appointed in May, 1775?
2 What victories did he achieve in 1776?
3 Explain why 1777 was a bad year for Washington.
4 Which two events helped the rebels in 1777–8?
5 What victory ensured final success for the Americans?
6 Who became the first president of the U.S.A.? When was this?

B. Make a neat copy of the diagram.

C. Write about: Saratoga, Trenton, Valley Forge, Yorktown.

D. Write a life story of George Washington.

# The American Constitution

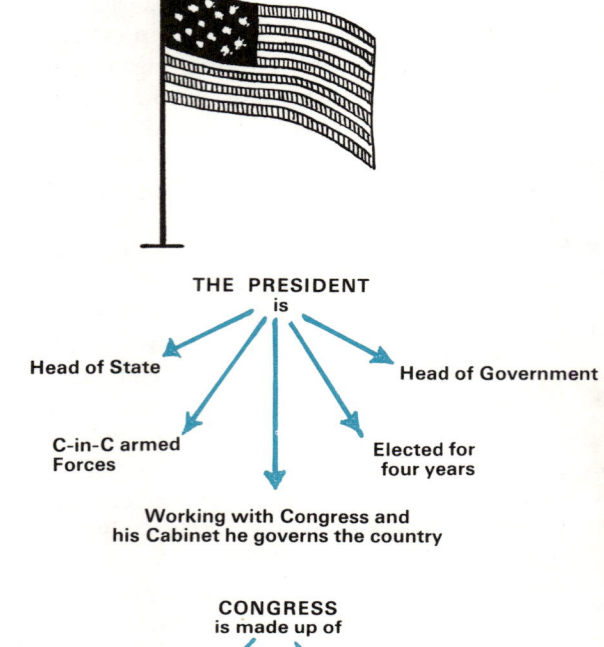

**THE PRESIDENT**
is

Head of State

Head of Government

C-in-C armed Forces

Elected for four years

Working with Congress and his Cabinet he governs the country

**CONGRESS**
is made up of

**THE SENATE**
Two senators from each state
A senator serves for six years

**THE HOUSE OF REPRESENTATIVES**
From each state on population basis
serve for two years

Congress is the law-making body

**THE SUPREME COURT OF JUSTICE**

Nine Judges chosen by President
The 'Watchdogs' of the Constitution

Pennsylvania State House (now known as Independence Hall) where the Constitutional Convention met in 1787

The American Constitution

# The American Constitution

The end of the war did not mean that the newly independent America's problems were also solved. The new nation contained people of widely differing classes and occupations, whose political opinions varied greatly. Some were loyal to the old Tory connections with England, some were the backwoodsmen of the frontier lands and some were the enslaved negroes of the South. There were no longer any British officials to take the responsibility of government, nor could disputes be sent to London. The nation consisted of a number of individual states whose assemblies alone had made their decision to fight the revolutionary war. The American Congress had merely been a gathering of state representatives and was not, in fact, a government for the whole nation.

Any idea of a strong central government which might limit the powers of the separate states faced strong opposition in the state parliaments. However, a handful of leaders, like George Washington, Alexander Hamilton and Benjamin Franklin, realised that America must have a strong central government if she were to avoid breaking up into a quarrelling group of little republics. A Convention was called together in Philadelphia in May, 1787 to work out a constitution for the American States.

The fifty-five members of the Convention agreed that the new Congress or American parliament must have the right to pass laws on all matters of national concern such as taxation, international trade, common defence and general welfare. They also agreed that the individual states, though freely able to run their own domestic concerns, could not retain the sovereignty and independence which they possessed during the war period.

Thus the American Constitution came to be written and signed in 1787. It provided two assemblies for making laws—the House of Representatives, elected on the basis of population every two years, and the Senate, elected on the basis of two senators from each state for a period of six years. The executive power (or the power to carry out laws) was to be in the hands of a President, to be chosen every four years. His responsibility also included the appointing of a cabinet and judges, the power to make treaties and command the army and navy. A Supreme Court of Justice was also appointed, with the power to decide how the law should be interpreted.

The Constitution was written to bind together the separate states into one strong nation. It was so framed that it ensured the rights of each state and defended the liberty and freedom of every individual.

## Things to do

A. Answer these questions:
1 Why did America need a new constitution?
2 Name three American leaders of the time.
3 When did the Convention meet? Where?
4 Name four parts of the constitution.
5 What was it hoped that the constitution would do?
6 What powers were given to the President?

B. Make a neat copy of the diagram and explain the constitution in your own words.

C. Make a list of the main parts of the American government.

# Benjamin Franklin 1706–1790

Philadelphia

Born in Boston, but did most of his work in Philadelphia.

Spent most of his life in the printing trade.

Some of his most successful publications.

1756 Pennsylvania Hospital—one of many contributions made by Franklin to public service.

Experimented with a kite to show that lightning was a form of electrical charge.

Crossed to London to put the Colonists' case before the British government.

1778

Helped to persuade France to join America in the War of Independence.

He helped to draft the Declaration of Independence 1776 and the Constitution 1787.

# Benjamin Franklin 1706–1790

To rise from humble beginnings to fame and fortune has become the traditional American success story. No better example can be found than the life of Benjamin Franklin. One of the ten children of a Boston soap-maker, he was apprenticed to the printing trade and had mastered his craft by the age of seventeen. For a time he worked as a clerk in a store, but soon returned to printing, and set up in partnership with a friend in Philadelphia, a city which was to bring him both riches and reputation.

In 1729 he wrote a pamphlet on the *Necessity of a Paper Currency* and won contracts to print the currency for several states. He added further money-making ventures, publishing the *Pennsylvania Gazette* and *Poor Richard's Almanack*, which was printed annually from 1732 to 1757 and poured out advice year after year on the merits of hard work and clean living: 'Do not squander time for that is the stuff that life is made of.' In 1748 he became a partner in the printing firm of Franklin and Hall, which brought him an average profit of five hundred pounds a year for the next eighteen years.

Franklin was outstanding, not just because he made money, but because he brought the same flair for success to so many widely different activities. He was a great believer in social improvement and was responsible for the setting up of a public library in Philadelphia, as well as a paid police force and an efficient fire service. His interest in education led to the formation of the Academy of Philadelphia (1751) out of which grew the University of Philadelphia.

He still had time to win an international reputation in science and politics. His experiments and observations on electricity were printed in the *Gentleman's Magazine* of England and reported to the Royal Society of London, as well as being translated into French, German and Italian.

Above all, he was practical, with a love of making things and experimenting. He had a hand in the invention of the lightning conductor, bifocal spectacles, a copying machine, a harmonica, a ship's anchor and a tool for removing library books from high shelves. The draughts whistling around his room caused him to invent the Franklin stove which circulated hot air.

This was enough fame for any man, but one can still add a long career of public and political service. In the seventeen-fifties, he looked after the mails. In the seventeen-sixties he represented the colonies in London. He returned home in 1775 to attend the second American Congress and to help with the drafting of the Declaration of American Independence in 1776.

He next went to France to seek aid for the rebels and was much sought after as the 'hero of freedom' by diplomats, scientists and fashionable ladies. He succeeded in persuading France to join America and between 1778 and 1781, twelve thousand soldiers and three thousand sailors left France to support General Washington.

He stayed on in France after the end of the war to make trade treaties, to observe the ascent of the first balloon and to study hypnotism as a cure for disease. He returned to America to attend the Constitutional Convention of 1787. He died three years later and was given the most impressive funeral the city of Philadelphia had ever seen. He remained a great favourite in France where he was remembered as the man who 'snatched lightning from the skies and the sceptre from the tyrants'.

## Things to do

A. Answer these questions:
1 What city made Franklin famous?
2 What was his trade?
3 Name two of his publications.
4 Name four of his inventions.
5 What did he give to Philadelphia?
6 How did he help the rebel cause?

B. Make a neat copy of the diagram.

C. Tell the story of Benjamin Franklin in your own words.

# Gold Rush '49 California (1)

Great
Salt Lake
Desert
Humboldt R.
Desert
Sierra
Nevada
Coloma
San
Francisco
CALIFORNIA
Rocky
Mountains
South
Pass
Fort
Laramie
N. Platte
Platte R.
Great Plains
Council
Bluffs
St.
Joseph
Missouri
Independence

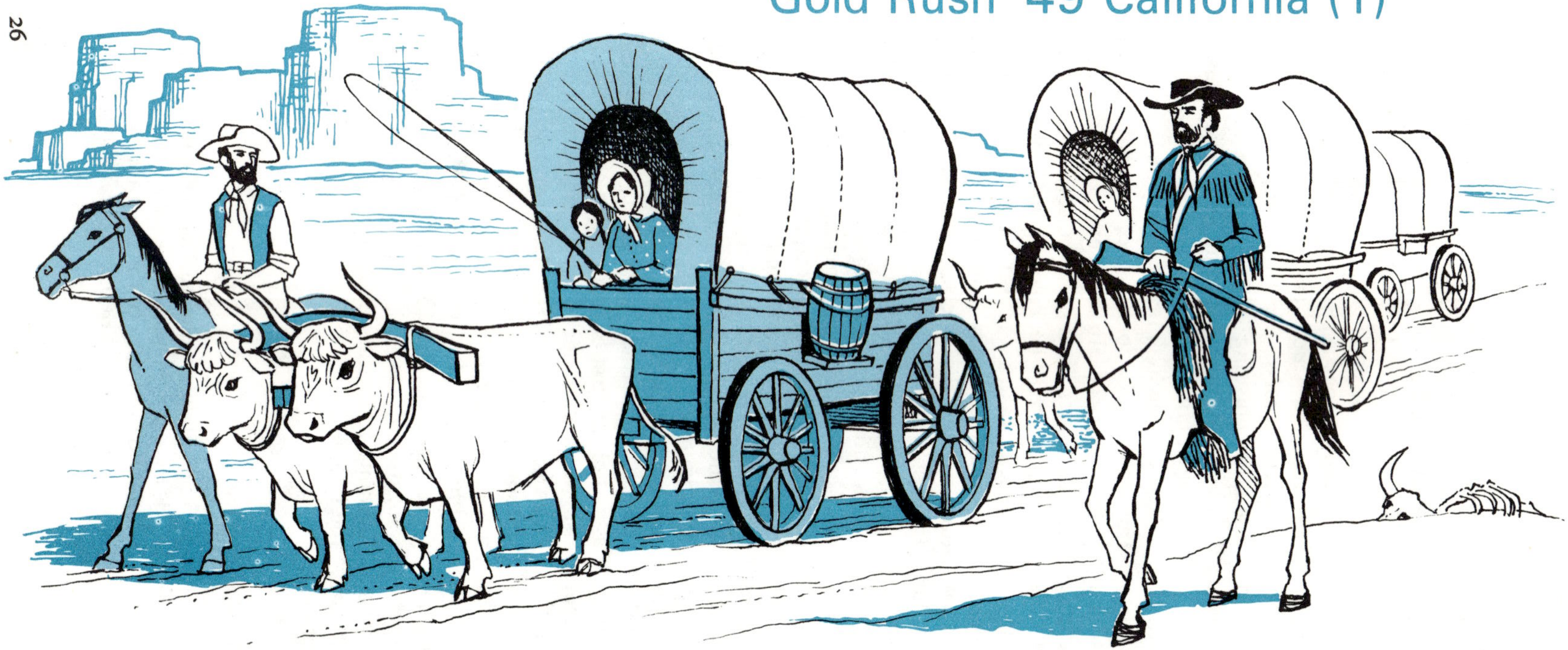

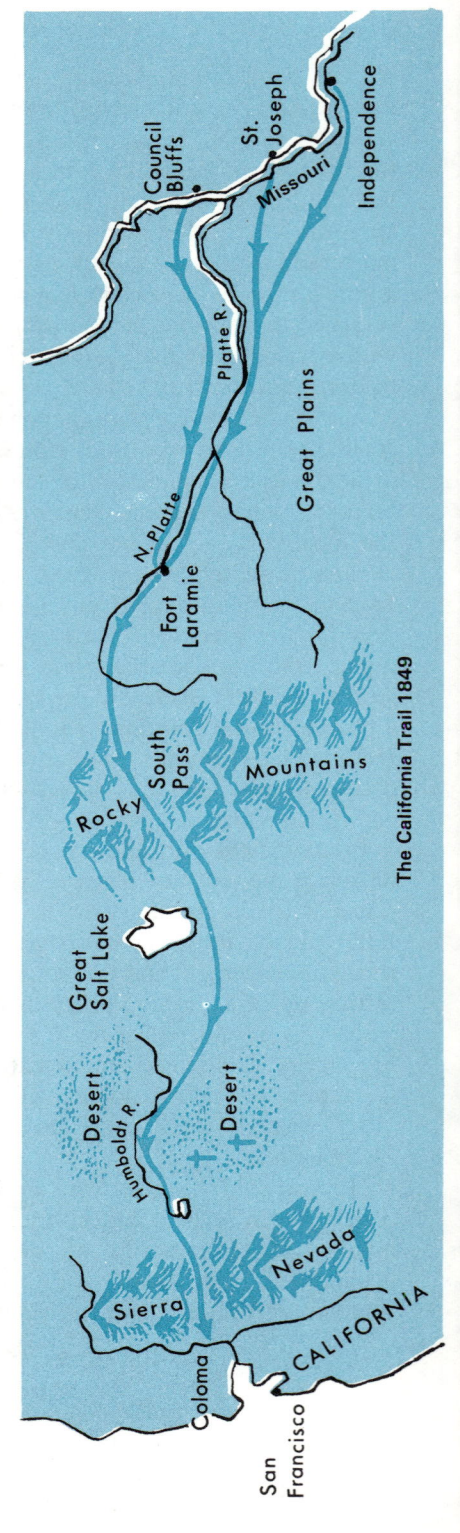

The California Trail 1849

# Gold Rush '49 California (1)

On March 15, 1848 the local newspaper, *The Californian,* carried a small item on an inside page which stated that gold had been found in the waters of Captain Sutter's mill-race at Coloma on the American river. Early in May, Sam Brannan ran through the streets of San Francisco waving a bottle of shining dust above his head and shouting, 'Gold! Gold! Gold! from the American river.'

So the rush began. San Francisco was emptied. Newspapers closed down. Hotels shut their doors. The crews of the ships in the harbour and the soldiers from the army deserted 'en bloc' and the military governor had to cook his own dinner. The blacksmith dropped his hammer, the farmer his sickle, the carpenter his plane, the baker his loaf. Every bowl, every tray, anything that would scoop up sand, rock and water, was taken off to the mines which were being dug on the banks of the American river. Tents were springing up on the hillsides and men could be seen bent down in the fiercest glare of the midday sun, washing for gold. Others, using the long cradle on rockers, were busy digging up the soil, filling the cradle, shaking it, washing away the earth and stones and hoarding their share of the yellow gold dust which they finally won from the black sand.

Four men could average one hundred dollars of gold a day. Someone found a piece of gold weighing eleven kilograms; others found nothing. One man gave away a large boulder flecked with gold which he used as a seat outside his tent. It was broken up and sold for three thousand dollars.

The news spread like ripples in a pond and people came in their thousands from all over America and even from Europe, urged on by the glowing account of the discoveries published in President Polk's annual Message, in which he stated that 'the abundance of gold in the area was of an extraordinary character'. The President wanted to fill up California's empty spaces with people and gold would act as a magnet.

Some came the long way round the Horn, others tried the short-cut across the disease-ridden isthmus of Panama to the Pacific and had to face cholera, yellow fever and malaria. A way was carved through the bandit-infested deserts of Mexico or through Arkansas and Texas, but the most popular route for the foreigners from Europe, the Americans from the north and for adventurers of all kinds, was the overland route across the continent.

The river town of St. Joseph was the starting point. Here you bought your mules for the mountains, your oxen for the prairies. You purchased a wagon specially strengthened for the long haul and freshly caulked to get across the rivers. It carried five persons, with a shot gun, pistols, horseshoe nails, axes and repair kit, stowed away in the trunk. You stocked up with flour, bacon, salt, sugar and coffee. You took cooking utensils, some spare clothes and boots, a pick and pan and maybe a mouth-organ.

You waited for the spring to melt the snows and the rains to make the prairies green with grass for the animals, and then you were ferried across the Missouri. The wild ones, the adventurers, the unwise, went their own way, sometimes to death in the deserts or on the frozen mountain side. The wise ones had organisation and discipline. Like the Charlestown Company, they planned the trip in detail, appointed a captain, quartermaster and lieutenants and they came through.

## Things to do

A.  Answer these questions:
  1  Name two events which started off the gold rush.
  2  Why was every bowl taken to the mines?
  3  What did President Polk state?
  4  Name four routes to the gold fields.
  5  Where did the overland route begin?

B.  Make a copy of the picture and describe two ways of getting the gold.

C.  Explain how the gold rush started and what happened first, or describe how you would have prepared for the overland journey to California.

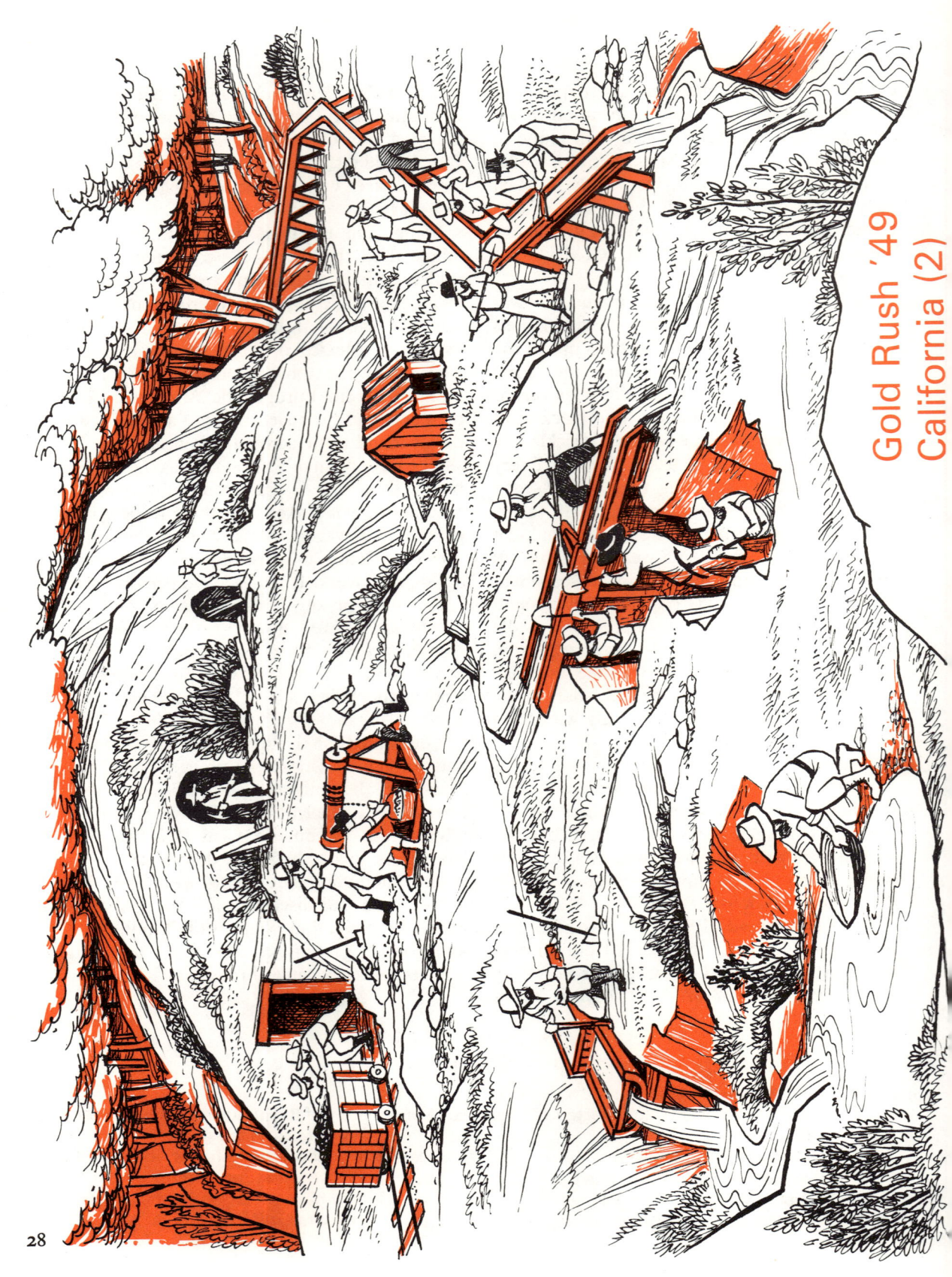

# Gold Rush '49 California (2)

In the first weeks they had grass, water and wood in plenty. They made fifteen miles (24 km) a day in teams of eight to ten wagons, following the rivers, the Little Blue, the Platte, the North Platte. When they were far from the salt licks and their bacon went rotten they could shoot the buffalo of the high plains. They floated their wagons across the wide rivers but the casualties through drowning were heavy.

At last they came to the Rockies and moved up through the South Pass. The traffic here was so heavy that the wheel ruts have left a permanent track in the frozen soil. Nine thousand feet (2743 m) up, facing ferocious storms and pushing ever uphill, they had to unload bedsteads, mattresses, trunks, harness, pots and pans, to keep moving forward.

Down the western side of the Rockies they rolled, to pick up the gleaming waters of the Humboldt river, only to find themselves by August in a temperature of one hundred and ten degrees in the shade (43°C.), with the river shrunk to a poisonous scum and sixty-five miles (104 km) of burning desert still to cross. It was here that some went mad. Others lay down to die among rusting metal, rotting food and the bones of mules and oxen. Their friends made crosses with sticks and pushed them into the sand to mark the place. They could not just leave them in this nowhere of a desert, so they invented names and laid their dead in 'Fortitude', 'Desolation' or 'Last Gasp'.

If the travellers survived the desert, the High Sierras towered above them. Here they risked freezing to death unless they got through before the September snows closed the passes. Marvellously, they did get through and in large numbers. By the end of 1849 forty to fifty thousand people had come into California and by 1852, the peak year of the gold boom, the state of California had two hundred and fifty thousand inhabitants, more than fifteen times the number living there in 1848. The gold was no myth either. In the best year over eighty million dollars' worth of gold was dug out of the area. This dropped to seventy million in 1854, but even as late as 1885 they were mining a steady twenty million dollars' worth a year in the 'Golden State'.

It was, however, the big businessmen who made the real fortunes. They had capital to buy expensive equipment, power and influence to hold on to claims and mines, and the skill to make money make more money. Leland Stanford, George Hearst and Collis P. Hartington, turned their gold into railroads, newspapers, universities, Old Masters, libraries and palaces. The little man, who bent over a pan or rocked the 'cradle' in the harsh sun, lost fortunes even more quickly than he discovered them. He was often glad to exchange his bag of gold for a return ticket home, though he might set up a store, become a saloon keeper, work for the stage coach or perhaps spend the rest of his life going wherever the rumour of gold called him.

The change in California was striking. In the winter of 1835 when the ship *Alert* called into the harbour of San Francisco, the bay was a picture of dreary sand dunes, high barren hills and a run-down mission. On Saturday, August 13, 1859 when the *Golden Gate* steamed in, her crowded passengers saw lighted streets, busy docks, clock towers and clipper ships, all part of a busy centre of commerce and a town of one hundred thousand people.

## Things to do

A. Answer these questions:
  1 Name four dangers the travellers faced.
  2 What proof is there that they 'got through'?
  3 Explain 'The gold was no myth.'
  4 Who made the real fortunes?
  5 How did California change?
B. Make a copy of the picture and tell its story.
C. Describe your journey in 1849 from St Joseph to California as a member of a wagon team.

# To Help You Remember

The Spaniards arrive in the South West.

The French come to the St. Lawrence and to the Mississippi—16th and 17th centuries.

17th century
The English come to Virginia and Cape Cod.

The Indians roam the Great Plains.

1775 – 1783
The War of Independence

George Washington—Commander-in-Chief, American Forces, 1775–1783

George Washington—President, U.S.A., 1789–1796

The President
The Congress
Supreme Court

The American Constitution

Pennsylvania Gazette

Poor Richard's Almanack

The Stars and Your Health

1706 — 1790

Benjamin Franklin—printer, social worker, scientist, politician, ambassador

1849

California—Gold Rush

# To Help You Remember

In the sixteenth century the S........ came to A...... to look for g..d. Cortes conquered M....o. Ponce de Leon sailed to F...... and De Soto and his men were the first Europeans to see the M........i. One of the strangest Spanish stories linked together E....., the slave, M....., the friar, and F....... C......, nobleman and army officer. The Spanish priests, Father K... and Father S.... came to America to convert the people to C.........y.

The French sent J...... C....., C......., and the Count de la S.... to explore the river St. L....... and the interior of C...a. Cartier is remembered because of his voyages up the St. L......e. C....... is famous as the founder of Q.... and La S....'s fame rests on his noteworthy voyage down the M.......... to the G.... of M....o.

Three ships sent out by the L..... Company sailed to C........ Bay and up the J.... river where they set up the colony of J........ in 16... The settlement was saved by Captain J... S.... and by the growing of t.....o.

The P...... F...... set sail from P....... in the 'M........' in September, 16.. to find a new home in N.... A.....a. They set up the colony of P....... which later became part of M............ and the first of the four N.. E...... colonies.

The Dutch laid the foundations of the modern city of N.. Y... which they called N.. A.......m. They employed an Englishman, H.... H..... in 1609 to sail to North America where he explored N.. Y... Bay and the river H....n. Famous Dutch families such as the V.......... and the R.........

had considerable influence on American history. The English took over the Dutch territory in 16.. and re-named it N.. Y... and N.. J....y. Thirteen colonies were built up on the east coast of N..·.. A...... by the E....h. They included five p........ colonies, four N.. E...... settlements and four m..... colonies.

The H... P.... were the home of the I.....s. The h.... and the b..... were two animals vital to their way of life.

A quarrel broke out between B...... and A...... between 17.. and 17... The S.... Act of 17.., the B..... M....... of 17.. and the B.... T.. P.... of 17.., all led up to the outbreak of the War of A....... I.......... of 17.. to 17...

George Washington was an officer in the Virginian army and the owner and manager of the M.... V..... estate. He was C........ in Chief of the A....... forces from 17.. to 17... After the war he helped to work out a c.......... for America and became the first American P....... in 17... He held this office until 17... There are four main parts to the American constitution: the P........, the S....., the House of R.............. and the S...... Court of J.....e.

Benjamin Franklin was a most unusual man in that he was successful at so many different things. He was a well-known p.....r, a great public servant to the town of P..........., a celebrated s.......t, a popular a........ and an efficient p........n.

Gold was discovered in C........ in 18... The people who made the real fortunes were L..... S......., G..... H..... and C..... P. H........n.

## Things to do

Write out the above passage in your note-book filling in the blanks. You will find the necessary information on the opposite page and in the earlier chapters of the book.

# The Causes of the American Civil War

Slaves picking cotton

1859

Harper's Ferry, Virginia: John Brown seized government arsenal. Hanged.

Who should hold the power? Central government or individual state?

Nov. 1860

Republican candidate, Abraham Lincoln, won Presidential election.

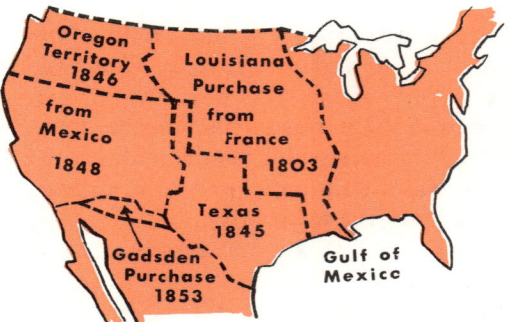

The addition of new states to the Union threatened to extend the conflict over slavery.

Feb. 1861

The Confederacy was set up, with its own flag and President.

By Harriet Beecher Stowe, it condemned slavery and sold millions of copies.

The bombardment of Fort Sumter, April, 1861

# The Causes of the American Civil War

The quarrel between the northern and southern states of America, which ended in Civil War, arose because the northern states believed that negro slavery should be forbidden in every state. The southern states, on the other hand, maintained that negro slaves were essential to do the work on the southern plantations. The southern states decided to break away from the north, but the northern states said that the Union must be held together and that no single state or group of states had the right to go their own way. So the war was fought over two points—negro slavery and the Union of the American states.

Negro slaves had been used to work on the plantations of the South since the seventeenth century. Slavery had died out in the North and it was hoped that it would disappear in time in the South. But the invention of a simple machine for cleaning cotton by Eli Whitney in 1793 made cotton the major crop of the South and the demand for slaves increased. The opening up of new territories in the West and the admission of new states to the Union threatened to increase the practice of slavery and make the problem worse.

The government tried to keep a balance in the Union between 'free' and 'slave' states but the quarrel over slavery became more and more heated. The sight of government troops capturing runaway slaves, in accordance with the Fugitive Slave Act of 1850, provoked riots in many towns. The novel *Uncle Tom's Cabin* —which told the story of the pious, patient slave, Uncle Tom, the white child Eva, who befriended him, and the villainous slave master, Simon Legree—was seen as a masterpiece in the North and condemned in the South as not giving a fair or true picture.

Violence broke out in Kansas between rival gangs calling for slavery or abolition of slavery. At Harper's Ferry in Virginia John Brown seized the government arsenal in 1859, hoping, with his supporters, to make this the first move in a campaign to wipe out slavery. He was captured by government troops and hanged, though many people regarded him as a martyr.

The Republican party had been formed in 1854 to oppose the spread of slavery. Its supporters were in the North and the Democrats were the party of the South. When the Republican candidate, Abraham Lincoln, won the presidential election in November, 1860 this was the last straw for the South. In December, 1860 South Carolina broke away from the Union and was followed by Mississippi, Alabama, Florida, Georgia, Louisiana and Texas. Delegates from these states met at Montgomery, Alabama in February, 1861 and set up the Confederate states of America with their own flag and their own president, Jefferson Davis.

The Civil War began in April, 1861 when Confederate guns in Charleston harbour, South Carolina, bombarded Fort Sumter and forced Major Anderson, the Union commander, to surrender. President Abraham Lincoln called for volunteers to fight the South and this brought Virginia (excluding West Virginia), Arkansas, Tennessee and North Carolina into the Confederate camp.

## Things to do

A. Answer these questions:
1. Why did North and South quarrel?
2. Why did slavery threaten to spread?
3. Name four things which made the quarrel more bitter.
4. What was the 'last straw' for the South?
5. Which states left the Union?

B. Make a neat copy of the diagram.

C. Write about: Eli Whitney, *Uncle Tom's Cabin*, John Brown, Abraham Lincoln.

D. Explain why the Civil War broke out.

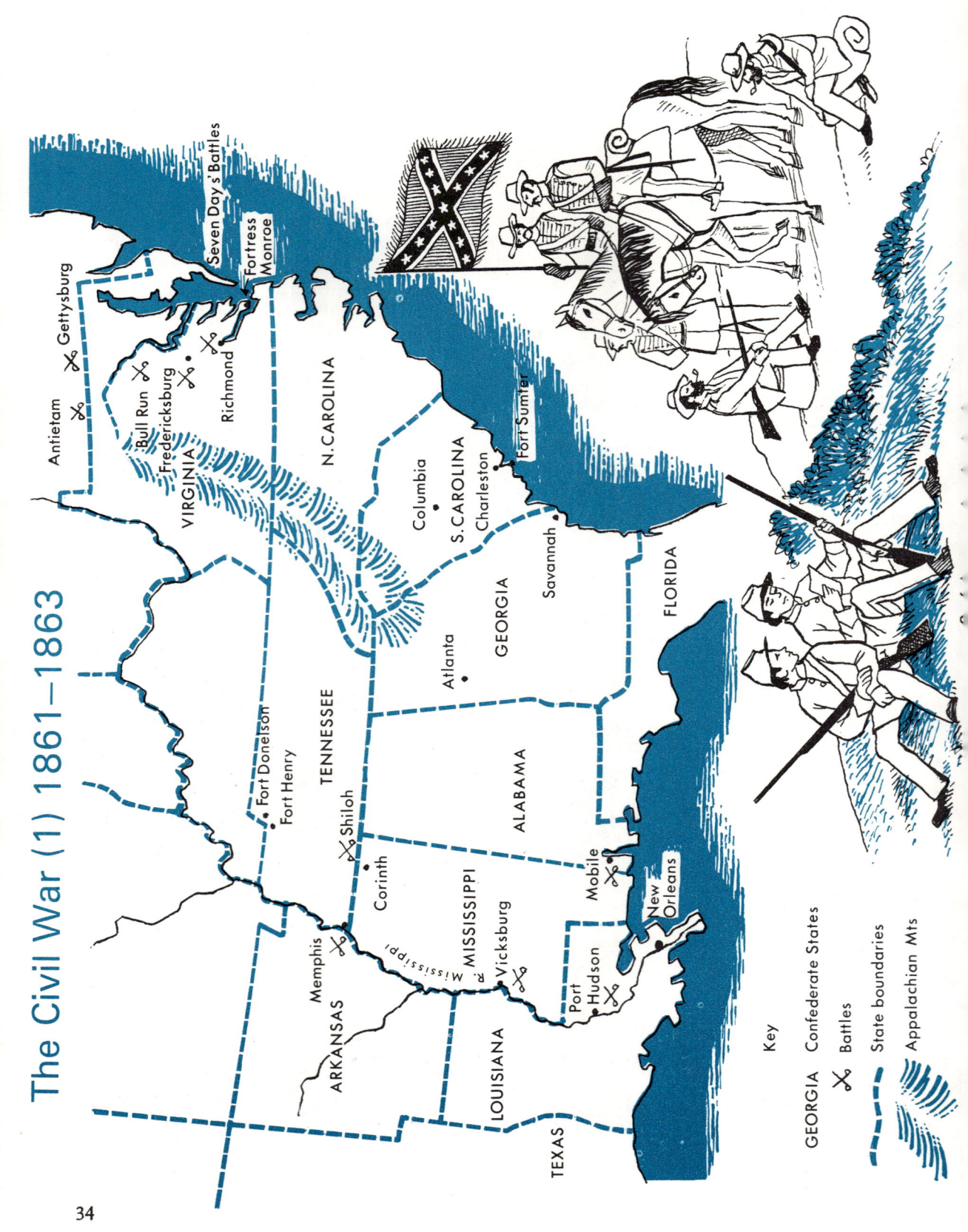

# The Civil War (1) 1861–1863

Antietam

Gettysburg

Seven Day's Battles

Fortress Monroe

Bull Run

Fredericksburg

Richmond

VIRGINIA

N. CAROLINA

Columbia

S. CAROLINA

Charleston

Fort Sumter

Savannah

GEORGIA

FLORIDA

Atlanta

Fort Donelson

Fort Henry

TENNESSEE

Shiloh

Corinth

ALABAMA

Mobile

New Orleans

Memphis

ARKANSAS

R. Mississippi

MISSISSIPPI

Vicksburg

Port Hudson

LOUISIANA

TEXAS

Key

GEORGIA   Confederate States

⚔   Battles

State boundaries

Appalachian Mts

34

# The Civil War (1) 1861–1863

The Northern or Union forces were supported by twenty-three states, as compared with eleven for the South. They had much the larger population behind them and nearly all of the vital war industries, such as coal, iron and steel, were in their control. They had the use of two-thirds of the American railway system and by far the greater part of the American navy and merchant marine. The war should therefore have been over quickly, but the South had some advantages. They were fighting on their own soil and defending their own homes. They had the best generals in Robert E. Lee and Stonewall Jackson and fine horsemen to make a superb force of cavalry. However, the longer the war went on, the more strongly would the superior industrial power of the North influence the final result.

Because of the Appalachian Mountains the war had to be fought on two fronts, one to the east and one to the west of the mountain barrier. On the eastern front the obvious target for the Union forces was the Confederate capital of Richmond. They made their first move in July, 1861 when they attacked a small Confederate force at Bull Run Creek, but they were driven back. President Abraham Lincoln appointed a new general, George B. McClellan, and in January, 1862 ordered him to advance on Richmond. The Union forces were taken by sea to Fortress Monroe and landed on the peninsula between the York and James rivers, with the object of attacking Richmond from the south. General McClellan was very cautious and he waited so long before taking action that General Lee took the initiative and attacked the Northern forces in the Seven Days' Battles. McClellan was forced to move back from Richmond in disgrace and defeat.

General Lee now felt confident enough to strike at Washington, the federal capital, and in September, 1862 he invaded Maryland to fight the battle of Antietam Creek. This was a setback for him. His advance to the north was checked but he won a victory at Fredericksburg in December, 1862. He continued to out-manœuvre the Union forces with further successes around Chancellorsville in May, 1863. The death of General Stonewall Jackson, killed in action, was a serious blow for the South.

On the west side of the mountains the Mississippi was the vital supply line for the Confederate armies and the obvious point of attack for the Union armies. By February, 1862 General Grant, the Union Commander, had captured Forts Henry and Donelson and though the Confederate forces re-grouped and counter-attacked at Shiloh, the Union troops had taken Corinth and Memphis by June, 1862. The North now controlled the Mississippi as far south as Vicksburg. A naval expedition captured New Orleans in May, 1862, leaving the city in flames, and the only part of the river left to the Confederate forces was the stretch between Vicksburg and Port Hudson.

Vicksburg was vital to the Confederate forces as a storehouse of food and armaments which came from the western states and from Europe by way of Mexico and Texas. It was a natural fortress situated on high land and set General Grant a tough problem. He started to attack it in the autumn of 1862. He drove off a local Confederate force and switched his offensive to the south of the town. Here he hammered away until the destruction inflicted by his guns and the starvation caused by his blockade forced the city to surrender in July, 1863. A few days later Port Hudson fell. It was the last Southern stronghold on the river. 'The father of waters now goes unvexed to the sea,' said Lincoln.

## Things to do

A. Answer these questions:
  1 What advantages had the North?
  2 What advantages had the South?
  3 Why was the war fought on two fronts?
  4 Who made the better start on the east?
  5 Who made the better start on the west?
  6 Name two of General Lee's successes.
  7 Name two of General Grant's successes.

B. Make a neat copy of the map of the Civil War.

C. Write about: General Lee, General Grant, Antietam Creek, Vicksburg.

D. Describe the main events in the Civil War between 1861 and 1863.

# The Civil War (2) 1863–1865

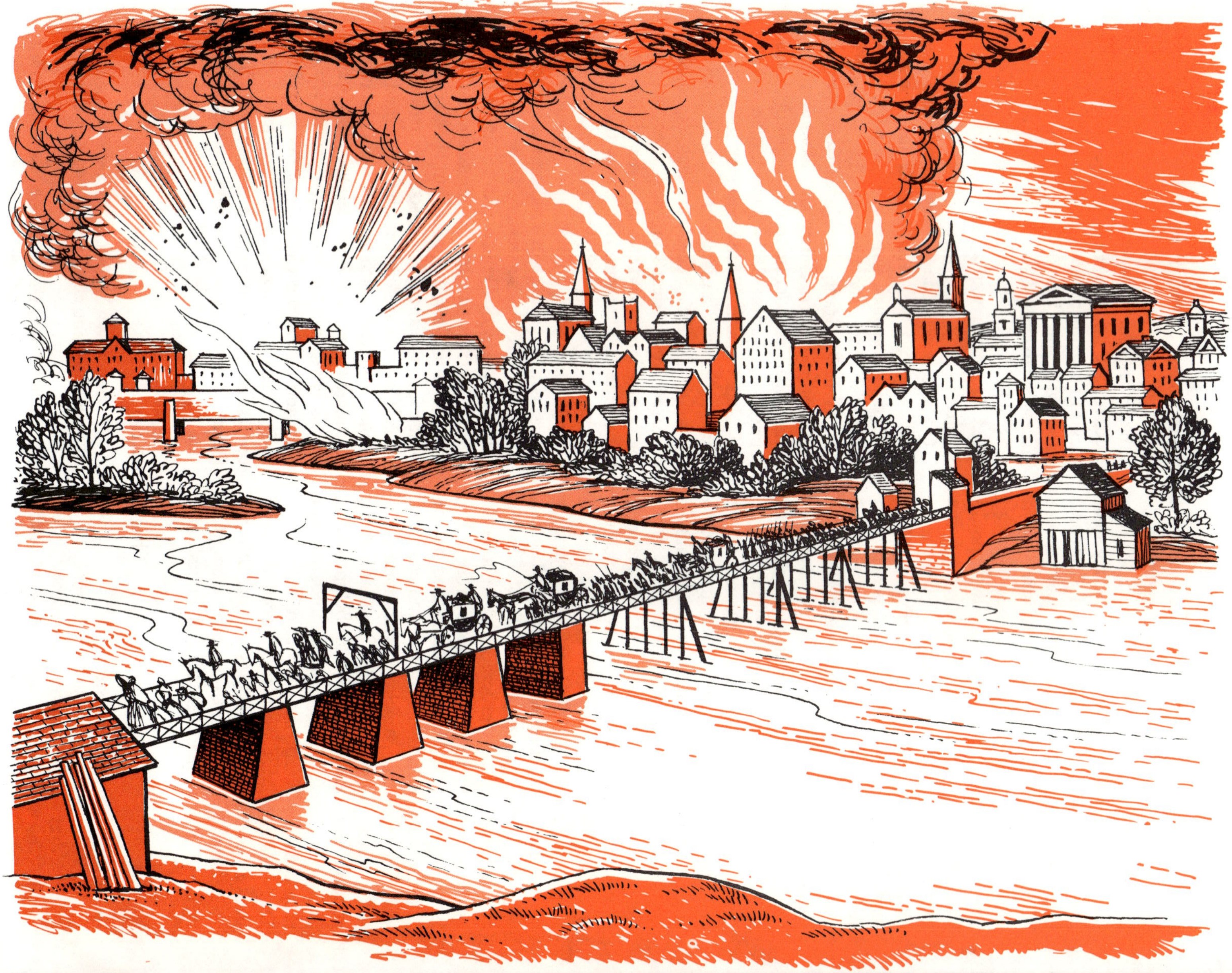

# The Civil War (2) 1863–1865

A long war could not favour the South and in the summer of 1863, General Lee decided to strike again at Washington. A victory here could bring a favourable peace for the Confederacy. He crossed the Potomac river in June, 1863 and gathered his seventy thousand men around the town of Gettysburg. The battle against the Union forces commanded by General Meade began on July 1. The first two days of violent fighting were indecisive and on the third day General Lee gambled on a frontal attack against the centre of the Union line, using the cream of his forces under General George E. Pickett, to storm Cemetery Ridge. The Confederate forces took the Ridge but could not hold it against heavy counter-attacks. General Lee lost one third of his army and was lucky to get the remainder away. Gettysburg and Vicksburg were two mortal blows for the South.

Four months later President Lincoln was asked to visit the battlefield and dedicate it as a national cemetery. He delivered his famous Gettysburg address: 'Fourscore and seven years ago (1776) our fathers brought forth on this continent a new nation conceived in liberty and dedicated to the proposition that all men are created equal. Now we are engaged in a great civil war testing whether this nation can long endure.'

In March, 1864 General Grant was put in charge of all Union forces, which he was able to unite in a common effort. A combined land and naval force was mounted to attack the port of Mobile, Alabama, one of the last southern ports through which supplies could be brought to Confederate forces. General Sherman was sent off on a drive to the south-east to destroy Southern morale and to split their forces. General Grant returned to Virginia to put pressure on Richmond and the Confederate forces under General Lee.

In the summer of 1864, General Sherman forced his way into Georgia and drove the Confederate troops out of Atlanta (September 1864). The way was now open to the Atlantic and Sherman pressed on, destroying anything of use to the Confederacy—cattle, crops, houses, railways, factories and towns. Savannah fell in December, 1864, 'a Christmas present for the President,' said the general, as he moved forward into North and South Carolina, leaving Charleston and Columbia in ruins. In April, 1865 Confederate forces surrendered in North Carolina.

From the summer of 1864 until the spring of 1865, General Grant mounted attack after attack on Richmond and on General Lee's Confederate army which defended both Richmond and Petersburg with magnificent skill and courage. Gradually the weight of numbers and the superiority of Union resources began to tell. In April, 1865 Richmond fell, and Lee trying to make his way to North Carolina with the last of his forces, found his way blocked by Union troops. He surrendered to Grant on April 9, at the Appomattox Court House in Virginia.

There was a presidential election in 1864. Lincoln called for 'no peace without Union', though he showed greater generosity to the South than his rivals. He won the election, helped in the autumn of 1864 by the fall of Atlanta and a spectacular naval victory in Mobile Bay. Once the fighting stopped, Lincoln was prepared to accept the rebel states back into the Union provided they took a simple oath of allegiance to the federal government. His assassination on April 14, 1865, believed to have been planned by Southern extremists, unfortunately put an end to any hope of an easy peace for the South.

## Things to do

A. Answer these questions:
   1. Name two mortal defeats for the South in 1863.
   2. Who took over Union forces in 1864?
   3. Where did Union forces strike in 1864?
   4. When and where did Lee surrender?
   5. What happened to President Lincoln?

B. Make a neat copy of the picture and tell its story.

C. Write about: Gettysburg, General Grant, General Sherman.

D. Describe how final victory went to the North between 1863 and 1865.

# The Early Railways

Boston
Troy
Albany
Buffalo
New York
Pittsburgh
Philadelphia
Baltimore
Richmond
Charleston
Chattanooga
Atlanta
Cincinnati
Chicago
St. Louis
Memphis
R. Mississippi

# The Early Railways

Railways made their appearance in America at about the same time as in England and for the same reasons—to carry heavy materials like coal or stone more cheaply and quickly than by canal or road. The first railways consisted of wagons pulled by horses along rails made of iron or wood. In 1826 horses pulled wagonloads of stone along the three miles of the Massachusetts Granite Railway and four years later were hauling passengers on the Baltimore and Ohio line.

George Stephenson's success with the 'Rocket' in England inspired the first steam-driven, wood-fired American locomotive which puffed out of Charleston in South Carolina in 1831. Three years later the line had been extended to Savannah, one hundred and sixty-five miles (265 km) away, the longest railway in the world at that time.

Helped by grants of land from the government, the railways expanded rapidly and by 1860 important railway lines ran from Boston via Troy and Albany to Buffalo, from Philadelphia via Pittsburgh to Chicago, from Baltimore through Cincinnati to St. Louis. In the south the railway linked Richmond to Chattanooga and Memphis and connected Charleston to Atlanta. New York was joined to Buffalo via Albany and to Boston via Troy.

There were many problems in the early days. Engines were overloaded and failed to climb some of the steeper routes. They came off the tracks because of snow or sand, cows or buffaloes. Before the introduction of Morse's electric telegraph it was difficult to know exactly where the trains were.

The passengers who crowded on to the new wonder had a rough ride. The seats were hard and there were no washing facilities or toilets. In summer, dust, sparks, cinders and smoke came through the windows. In winter the only heat came from the red-hot stove placed in the middle of the aisle. The passengers sat in pairs on each side of the aisle which stretched the full length of the coach. If you were near the stove you were roasted, if far away, you froze. There were no dining cars but you might get a ten minutes' stop to gobble 'coarse coffee and putty pies'.

At each halt on the long runs the aisle would be invaded by 'newsboys' who sold newspapers, sweets, tobacco, fruits, nuts and patent medicines. Some of the 'newsboys' stayed on the train and dropped their goods in your lap, hoping that you would buy and the long journey would bring them rich sales. From such humble beginnings, Tom Taggart, U.S. senator and hotel owner, and A. Brady, fight promoter and theatrical producer, went on to make their fortunes.

George M. Pullman was responsible for a revolution in railway comfort in the last quarter of the nineteenth century. He provided high quality sleeping and dining cars, parlour cars for the daytime and observation cars from which to admire the passing scenery. The interior fittings of the cars were lavish and included electric lighting, plush seats, carpeted floors, rich curtains and mahogany furniture. The use of coal and of the Westinghouse airbrake, together with the universal adoption of the electric telegraph, helped to make the railways safe and fast, as well as comfortable.

Freight was as vital as passengers to the growth and prosperity of the railways and the new territories through which they passed. Corn and cattle, wheat and pigs came in great quantities by rail to the eastern seaboard, while manufactures of all kinds—calico, cutlery, boots, hats, farm tools and machinery, fencing and fertilisers, glass and hardware—passed them going in the opposite direction from east to west.

## Things to do

A. Answer these questions:
   1 When did railways first appear in America?
   2 Why were they built?
   3 Name two early railways.
   4 Name three main lines built by 1860.
   5 How did Morse help the early railways?
   6 What did Pullman introduce?

B. Make a neat copy of the diagram.

C. Describe a journey on an early American railway.

# Railways—Crossing a Continent

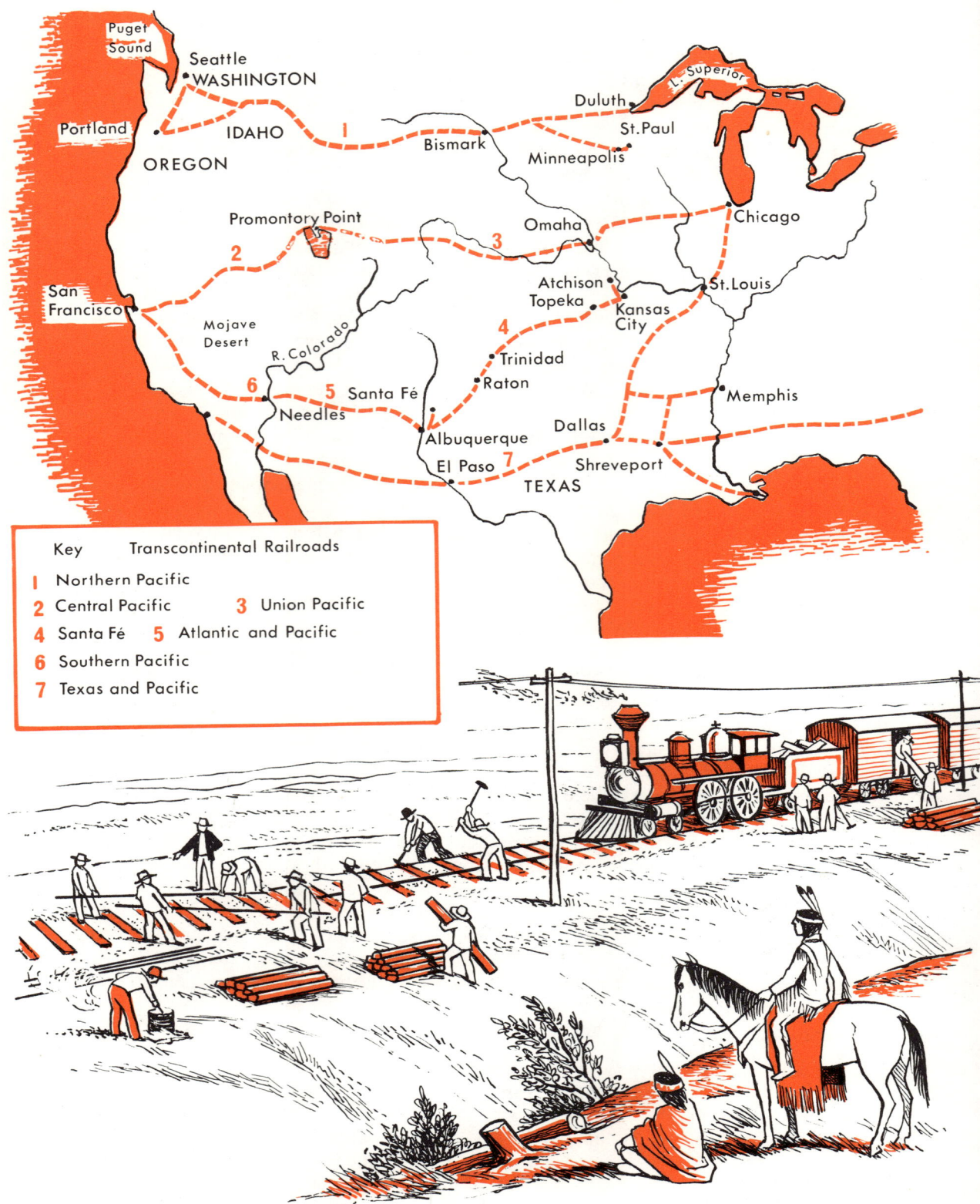

**Key      Transcontinental Railroads**

**1** Northern Pacific

**2** Central Pacific      **3** Union Pacific

**4** Santa Fé      **5** Atlantic and Pacific

**6** Southern Pacific

**7** Texas and Pacific

Building the Transcontinental Railroads

# Railways—Crossing a Continent

In 1862 and 1864 Congress passed the Pacific Railroad Acts. This encouraged the private railroad companies to make a start on the long-awaited construction of a trans-continental railway to link the east and west coasts of America. The Central Pacific Company from San Francisco and the Union Pacific from Omaha agreed to work towards each other as fast as they could in order to complete the first American trans-continental railway. Work began on the Californian side in 1864 and on the eastern side in 1866. Land was made available and sixteen thousand dollars was paid for every mile (1·6 km) of track laid.

The Union Pacific had the easier task, since their route was flatter and they had an unbroken supply line back to the river Missouri. The Central Pacific had some very difficult territory to cross and much of their material had to come by the long sea journey around the Horn. Both companies employed thousands of men and animals and vast quantities of rails, timber, food, fuel and bridging.

The eastern group worked their way over the Rockies. The western company climbed the High Sierras. Then they both worked like fury to get as far as they could before the two tracks met, for every mile laid counted in hard cash. The tracks met on May 10, 1869, at Promontory Point, Utah. Chinese crews for the Central, and Irish teams for the Union, had together laid 1,775 miles (2855 km) of line.

The great moment of completion had to be properly celebrated. The governor of California, Leland Stanford, stood ready to drive the golden spike into the last sleeper. The band stopped playing. The crowd of onlookers was silent. The telegraph operator high up on his pole was connected to San Francisco and New York. The governor lifted his hammer, gave a mighty swing and missed—but the news of completion had flashed along the wire and New York City fired a salute of one hundred guns.

Other continental railways quickly followed. The Northern Pacific was authorised by the government to run from Lake Superior to Puget Sound. It was started by Jay Cooke who took it as far as Bismarck before he went bankrupt. It was taken on by Henry Villard, who pushed it through to Portland (1883) and Seattle (1887).

In the south the Santa Fé Railroad started from Atchison in Kansas, continued through Topeka to Trinidad, Colorado, then went over the Rockies and down to Albuquerque and Santa Fé. The Atlantic and Pacific Railroad, a subsidiary of the Santa Fé, ran the next stretch to Needles on the Colorado river, and an agreement with the Southern Pacific took the line across the Mojave desert and into San Francisco.

Railway agents scoured Europe for settlers and whisked them off to the western plains, offering cheap fares and land at one dollar an acre. The immigration department of the Santa Fé Railroad transported ten thousand Germans to Kansas in 1874, and the Northern Pacific brought settlers to isolated Oregon, Washington and Idaho.

The railways which were the wonder of the nineteenth century gave way to new kinds of transport in the twentieth century. Growing competition from the motor-car, or 'automobile', the heavy goods vehicle, the passenger coach and the aeroplane, caused a sharp fall in railway construction and use. From 1870 to 1920 the total railway mileage in the U.S.A. increased by five times. From 1920 the decline in construction became more and more marked until by 1970 half of the nineteenth century track had been pulled up and what was left was underused, at less than fifty per cent capacity.

## Things to do

A. Answer these questions:
  1 How did Congress encourage the railway companies?
  2 Which two companies started the work?
  3 Where did the tracks meet? When?
  4 Name four trans-continental railroads. Why were these railroads important?

B. Make a neat copy of the map and picture.
C. Tell your story of the construction of the Central Pacific and Union Pacific Railroads.
D. Describe the growth of the railways and show why they were important.

# Cowboys and Cattlemen

Kansas City

MISSOURI

Mississippi

Abilene

Ellsworth

Wichita

ARKANSAS

INDIAN TERRITORY

Dodge City

1 Fort Worth

TEXAS

2

San Antonio

LOUISIANA

3

Rio Grande

MEXICO

**Key**

Railroads

Cattle Trails

1 Chisholm Trail

2 Western Trail

3 Goodnight – Loving Trail

# Cowboys and Cattlemen

The famous Texan Longhorn cattle could be bought in Mexico, taken across the Rio Grande river, driven across the American plains to the more northerly cities and sold for a large profit. In the eighteen-forties, cattle bought for five to fifteen dollars each in Texas, could be sold for more than four times that amount if walked north along the trails to California, Missouri, Ohio and Kansas. The cowboys who drove the cattle brought a new way of life with them which spread across the plains as far north as Nebraska, Colorado, Wyoming and Montana.

The Civil War stopped the cattle drives. Cowboys were called up. Trails were blocked and markets cut off, but the end of the war led to the greatest cattle boom of the century. By 1866 with the herds under control and the 'Confederate' cowboys looking for work, the cowmen were ready to drive the trails again. They were helped by the growth of the railways and by the genius of Joseph McCoy who worked to clear the trails, to relax the state laws against the cattlemen, and to provide a railhead at Abilene. Here they could be certain of selling their cattle at a good price for the markets of Chicago and St. Louis.

When McCoy looked at Abilene in 1867 it was a frontier village with a dozen log cabins, one hotel with six rooms, a blacksmith's shop, a general store and a saloon. A post by the side of the track marked the place where the trains stopped. McCoy built a cattle yard to hold one thousand cattle, a barn, an office, a three-storey hotel, a livery stable for horses and a bank. He contacted a local railroad company and obtained cheap rates for the shipment of his cattle to Chicago. He won over the support of the governor of Kansas and advertised his new 'cattle-town' throughout the West, telling the cattlemen on the trails to come to Abilene. This they did, and between 1867 and 1871 one and a half million cattle passed through Abilene, with another million each reaching Wichita, Ellsworth and Dodge City, as the railroad moved further west.

The cattlemen came up from Texas along the Chisholm trail by way of Fort Worth and Indian Territory to Abilene. On the western trail they passed through Dodge City and Ogallala and moved on to Nebraska, Wyoming and Montana. The most dangerous trail was the oddly-named Goodnight and Loving trail through Comanche territory to the extreme west. It was first travelled by two young men called Mr. Goodnight and Mr. Loving.

It was the danger and freedom of the open plains and dusty cattle trails which gave the cowboy his romantic character in fact and fiction. Ten-gallon hat, six-shooter, faithful horse, high-heeled boots, sparkling spurs and frilled chaps—he had all the trappings of a hero. The hardships and the dangers he faced were real enough: getting up at four in the morning, choked with dust behind a trail herd, swimming muddy and swollen rivers, pulling cows out of muddy bogs, freezing in winter and sweating in summer, with one eye watching for hostile Indians, for poisonous snakes which crept up on you at night and for the terrifying stampede that could start with the breaking of a twig or a clap of thunder.

He fought prairie fires, turned stampedes, rode the range, stood guard by night and day in good weather and bad, and never complained as long as he could do it all from the back of a horse. The only work on foot was roping or branding in the corral.

## Things to do

A. Answer these questions:
1 Why were the cattle taken north?
2 What stopped the drives?
3 Who helped them start again?
4 Name three ways he helped cattlemen.
5 Name three famous cattle trails.
B. Make a neat copy of the map and picture.
C. Write about Abilene, Joseph McCoy, Cattle Trails, Cowboys.

# Law and Order at Abilene

A frontier cattle town

44

# Law and Order at Abilene

When the Texas Longhorns arrived at Abilene they were sold to men like Joseph McCoy and shipped to Chicago and St. Louis. The cowboys were paid off and after long months on the trail they rushed into town to spend their money, to gamble, drink and fight.

In desperation the town fathers advertised for a marshal, but cattle towns, like mining towns, attracted a fair proportion of ruffians who drove the new marshal out of town. Theodore C. Hayes, the town chairman, would not give up and he offered the vacant post of law officer to Thomas James Smith of Colorado, ex-policeman and railway worker. Smith agreed to take on the job, but it was suggested that he should first look around the town. He walked down the main street, his sturdy figure casting a broad shadow, his red hair a bright target, his grey-blue eyes carefully searching the wooden sidewalks and the saloons.

He came back to the chairman's office, pinned on his badge and went out to that part of Abilene where the troublemakers gathered. So he met Big Hank, the meanest man in town, whose sinister six-shooter shone in its leather holster. Tom Smith politely asked for the weapon to be handed over, but all he received was abuse. The new marshal sprang at his adversary, and with hands toughened and hardened on the railway tracks, dropped Big Hank with a flurry of blows. He took Hank's gun and ordered him out of town.

The news swept around the saloons and through the cattle camps on the edge of the town. Into Abilene came Wyoming Frank, sure that he could defy the new marshal and his fancy laws. Straight to Kelly's saloon he went and the raw whisky made his boasting loud and surly. Tom Smith came quietly down the street. The saloon doors slapped against each other as Wyoming Frank came out to mock and sneer. Silently he was forced back into the saloon and the final blow thrust his insults down his throat as he struck the floor by the side of the bar. His gun was coolly taken from him and the astonished spectators meekly handed over theirs.

So Tom became boss of Abilene. He rode the town on his grey horse, 'Silver Wheels'. He neither drank nor gambled. He kept order without killing. He was respected. There was rarely any trouble now; only a newcomer, like the man in the cheap tavern on Texas Street, would dare to carry a gun. As Smith walked in someone grabbed the kerosene lamp from its bracket and hurled it at the law officer. Fortunately it did not explode, but it made the desperado's friends scatter and the marshal hauled him out and carried him across the street to the jail.

This happened in Abilene in the summer of 1870. Five months later Smith died, cornered, wounded and deserted by his deputy. The town closed its doors. The citizens stood silently as 'Silver Wheels' with his saddle empty followed the coffin to the cemetery.

They appointed another marshal, Wild Bill Hickok, to tame the Texas cattlemen. Six feet tall with a droopy moustache and hair down to his shoulders, he was a classy dresser who wore polished patent-leather cowboy-style boots with high heels and flowered silk waistcoats. With a pistol in each hand he could puncture the brim of a hat as it spun in the air, keep a tin dancing in the dust or put ten bullets through one small hole in a wooden post. It was Tom Smith, though, that they remembered. He had used his hands where Wild Bill needed his guns.

The blizzard of 1885–6, the greater importance of the settled farmer and the growing use of barbed wire closed up the cattle trails and made the cowboy and the marshal less important figures in the West.

## Things to do

A. Make a neat copy of the picture and write a few lines about the town and the people in it.

B. Tell Tom Smith's story in your own words or make up your own 'Western' based on any story or film familiar to you.

# The Last Years for the Indian

The Sun Dance, the Indians' annual religious festival. In this dance of endurance the men are attached to the Sacred Tree by strings pinned to their chests. Each movement is painful. The third man has just finished and sinks to the ground, scattering the ritual feathers which he holds in his hands.

# The Last Years for the Indian

The twenty-five years from 1865 to 1890 were years of tragedy for the American Indian. The end of the Civil War was followed by a great movement of people into his traditional homeland. Settlers in their thousands were carried by stage coach or railway, by covered wagon or on horseback. They came to find gold or silver, trail cattle or settle down and farm. They came from every part of America and from Europe as well. They wanted the West and they took it.

If you destroyed the buffalo you destroyed the Indian. Wagon trains, stage coach companies and the new railways hired professional hunters like 'Buffalo Bill' (William Cody) to shoot the buffaloes in vast numbers in order to provide meat for immigrant settlers and for railway workers. Behind the settlers and the hunters came more and more soldiers, sent to round up, tame, harass and kill the 'Redskins'. Government policy aimed to put the Indians into large camps away from their own lands, where they could live on the daily ration of beef and corn provided by the state.

The Sioux, one of the largest remaining Indian tribes, felt that their world was falling apart, for their land, their buffaloes and their freedom were all threatened. They refused to walk tamely into the reservations and preferred to fight, even to die, for the life of the free Sioux. They gathered together in the area of the Black Hills, a region sacred to the Indian, and for a century, rich in antelope, deer and buffalo. Unfortunately for them there was gold in the Black Hills and miners poured into Wyoming and Montana, followed by the army in the persons of General Custer and the Seventh American Cavalry.

In the summer of 1876, the Sioux Indians under their Chief, Sitting Bull, held their annual festival, the Sun Dance, on the banks of the Rosebud river. Sitting Bull had a dream. He saw the Bluecoats falling from the skies into the Sioux village where they were killed with ease. This, he was certain, forecast a great victory.

There was a first skirmish between the Americans and the Sioux on the Rosebud river and then Sitting Bull took his people westwards to the Little Big Horn. Here he placed fifteen hundred Indian warriors along the south bank of the river for a distance of four miles. Furthest upstream at the entrance to the Indian village were the Hunkpapa, covered as one moved downstream by the Blackfoot Sioux, the Sans Arc, the Oglalas, the Brulés and the Cheyenne.

General Terry, the commander of the American forces, decided on a three-pronged attack and told General Custer just to make a careful reconnaissance of the area. Custer, seeking the glory, went forward alone with the Seventh Cavalry, and on June 25, 1876, in the middle of a bright summer's day, he attacked the Indian village. He was killed and his force wiped out.

The Americans clamoured for revenge. The Indian tribes were harassed, broken up, driven into the mountains. Their chiefs were murdered and the final and awful humiliation came at the Battle of Wounded Knee in the winter cold of January 1891, when American cannon of the Seventh Cavalry killed two hundred men, women and children, and dug for them a common grave in the snow-covered ground. An Indian chief, just before his death, spoke an epitaph for all Indians. 'I don't want to settle. I love to roam the prairie but they cut my timber, killed my buffalo and broke my heart.'

## Things to do

A. Answer these questions:
  1 Why were the years 1865–90 bad for the Indians?
  2 Why did hunters shoot the buffaloes?
  3 What was government policy?
  4 Where did the Sioux win a victory?
  5 Where was their last defeat?

B. Make a neat copy of the picture and explain it in your own words.
C. Describe the last years of the Sioux.
D. Write about: Sitting Bull, the Black Hills, Battle of the Little Big Horn, Battle of Wounded Knee.

The New Americans
1860–1930

# The New Americans 1860–1930

This book began with the entry into America of Spaniards, Frenchmen and Englishmen who gave the U.S.A. its special character, its government, its language, its religion and its freedom. Some three hundred years later another wave of people flooded in from Europe, in numbers greater than ever before. They came as early as the eighteen-forties but between 1860 and 1900 fourteen million immigrants entered the U.S.A., to be followed by another eighteen million between 1900 and 1930—from Asia, Canada and Europe.

They were persuaded to leave their homes because of hard times or persecution, war or revolution, and also because they believed that America was the promised land of high wages, good jobs, and freedom to live one's life without fear. America needed cheap labour for her growing factories and steelworks and the railway companies were eager to settle people on the lands which they had acquired from the government. There were American agents at many points in Europe seeking emigrants.

The Irish needed little persuasion to leave the poverty of their famine-stricken land. Potatoes were their main food and farming their only livelihood. The blight which destroyed the potato crop of 1845 helped to urge one quarter of Ireland's population across the Atlantic. England's industry and farming went through hard times in the last quarter of the nineteenth century and so many people left England and Scotland, as well as Ireland, that the United Kingdom sent more people to the U.S.A. than any other country.

The Germans with their beer, brass bands and sausages, their hard work, discipline and good farming, settled in large numbers in the big cities between Pennsylvania in the east and Kansas in the west. Wars and revolutions in Europe, harsh governments—or just economic depression and the hope of better times across the sea—persuaded them to leave home. From northern Europe came the Swedes and Norwegians, hardy farmers well suited to the more severe climate of northern states such as Minnesota, Nebraska and the Dakotas. From eastern Europe came large numbers of Jews, especially from Poland and Russia. Persecution in their own countries made them listen eagerly to the American immigration agents who promised them both peace and riches.

From the eighteen-seventies and up to the early years of the twentieth century a growing number of newcomers poured in from south-eastern Europe. The Italians left a very poor and highly over-populated land. The Austrians and Hungarians came away from a decaying empire and the clouds of war, while Russia was going through the last years of the Czars and beginning to hear the first sounds of the Bolsheviks.

The emigrants travelled by rail from all over Europe to points of embarkation at Athens, Constantinople, Antwerp, Bremen and Hamburg. They travelled in cattle trucks with few comforts. Every hundred miles (160 km) or so they would draw into a siding to take on hopeful travellers—Russians, Poles, Serbs, Austrians, Hungarians, Italians, Lithuanians.

When they arrived at the port of embarkation they were gathered together so that they could clean themselves up, sort out their luggage and have their papers checked. Everyone had to have an exit paper, a spare twenty-five dollars, so as not to become a public charge, and the price of their passage. Because of a price war between the shipping companies the fare had dropped to between ten and twenty dollars a head. At last they were ferried out to the big ship and stowed away in the steerage accommodation, as many as nine hundred huddled together.

## Things to do

A. Answer these questions:
  1 When did the new Americans come?
  2 Why did they leave home?
  3 Make a list of the nations which sent people to America.
  4 How did they travel?
  5 What was every settler required to have?

B. Copy the picture and write about it.
C. Write your own account of the 'New Americans'.
D. Write an account of an emigrant family from the time they left home to the moment they boarded the ship.

'Streets Paved with Gold'

Give me your tired, your poor,
Your huddled masses yearning to breathe free,
The wretched refuse of your teeming shore.
Send these the homeless, tempest-tost to me.
I lift up my lamp beside the golden door.
Emma Lazarus 1849–1887

# 'Streets Paved with Gold'

As they walked on to the ship the city man carried a battered suitcase, the peasant a wicker basket, but for many, what little they had could be wrapped in a sheet or blanket. Some relic of the old home would be kept, a goosefeather pillow, a brass candlestick, an ikon, a lock of hair or a special petticoat. They were suspicious of foreign food and many carried a cooking pot, some raw vegetables and a hunk of sausage. For two weeks or eight days, depending on the size of the ship and the state of the weather, they sat and thought of their new life. They sewed. They played cards. They sang to keep their spirits up, accompanied by mouth-organ, tin whistle or accordion.

When they arrived in New York harbour the scene was one of bedlam. A milling throng of inspectors, wardens, doctors, nurses, interpreters, con men and all kinds of swindlers were all having their say at once, not to mention the frightened babble of the immigrants. No wonder some of the immigrants were labelled with the oddest of names for the rest of their lives. The medical examination was something to be feared. If you were marked with 'H' for heart disease, 'I' for the eye trouble common in Eastern Europe, or the circle and cross which stood for feeble-mindedness, then you were not allowed to stay in America. Eight out of ten survived the medical and passed on to questions about background, dependants and job prospects.

At last you had the coveted landing card in your hand. You visited a currency booth and exchanged your small pile of drachmas, roubles, marks or lire for the desired dollars. If you planned to go out West you were handed over to a travel agent or railroad man, who supervised the remainder of your journey.

If you were going to stay in or around New York, the representative of an aid society might help you; or one of the local political agents might assist you, hoping to secure another block of immigrant votes.

When the immigrants finally stepped on to the streets they did not find them paved with gold. Some exchanged hard times in the homeland for a baffling and brutal life in city slums, harsh factories, railway workshops or the sweatshops of local industry. Unwanted, it seemed, they huddled together in 'Little Italy', 'Little Russia' or 'Little Poland'.

Help often came from the neighbourhood political agent. He knew and befriended his local people for the sake of the one vital thing democracy had given them—a vote. A tenement house contained many families. Many tenements made up a city block. So many blocks made a precinct, so many precincts a ward, and all those votes could eventually decide the result of an election and the fate of a president, a congressman, a political party. Whoever won had a whole string of jobs to hand out, from humble doorman to haughty judge. So the neighbourhood politician, usually an Irishman or a Jew, would have a lot of influence. He could get you a job, save your son from jail, persuade the landlord to do the repairs and in time of distress bring food and medical care, in return for your vote.

However harsh the day-to-day conditions might be, the great attraction of America for the immigrant was the wonderful opportunity the country offered to rise from the humblest position to fame and fortune. In a booming America, Andrew Carnegie in steel, John D. Rockefeller in oil and Henry Ford in automobiles, were magic names for every immigrant.

## Things to do

A. Answer these questions:
   1 What did they bring from home?
   2 What did they do on board?
   3 Why did they pick up odd names?
   4 Who failed to get in?
   5 Why was life hard for some?
   6 Who gave help? Why?
   7 What was the real attraction for the immigrant?
B. Make a copy of the picture and write about the Statue of Liberty.
C. Imagine you are an immigrant and describe what happens to you from the time you get off the boat.

# The Inventors (1)

Singer 1856

Sholes 1867

Beil 1876

Edison

gramophone 1900

phonograph 1877

1879

electric storage battery

Eastman 1888

# The Inventors (1)

Alexander Graham Bell (1847–1922) was born in Edinburgh but his family moved first to Canada and later to the U.S.A. Like his father, he was deeply interested in the study of speech and its facial movements, with the object of helping the deaf to speak. In 1873 he became Professor of Speech and Sound at Boston University. In his spare time he worked with Thomas Watson, a young mechanic, on an apparatus for transmitting sound by electricity. This was the basis of the telephone. His invention was granted a patent in 1876 and was produced commercially by the Bell Telephone Company from 1877.

The handy and familiar 'Kodak' camera was the work of George Eastman (1854–1932) who invented the roll photographic film in 1884 and put his simple hand-held box camera on the market in 1888. The camera was sent back to the manufacturer for developing, printing and re-loading. In 1900 he brought out the 'Brownie' camera for children which sold at one dollar.

The first practical typewriter was built by Christopher L. Sholes in 1867. Six years later he signed a contract with E. Remington and Sons of New York to manufacture his machines, which were first put on the market in 1874, and became known as 'Remingtons'.

'Singer' has become the household name for sewing machines, which were invented as early as the eighteen-forties but first became commercially successful when Elias Howe and Isaac Singer pooled their ideas and their patents in 1856. By 1870 the American nation was buying half-a-million sewing machines a year and on easy payments.

The busiest inventor of them all was Thomas Alva Edison (1847–1931) who patented thirteen hundred inventions. Born in Ohio and brought up in Michigan, he was a railroad newsboy at twelve, a telegraph operator at fifteen, and the inventor of a vote-recording machine at nineteen.

Edison used his great scientific skill to tackle everyday problems and to invent simple appliances which could be mass-produced for the benefit of a very large number of people. His vote-recording machine worked well when it was demonstrated before Congress but nobody bought it. There was no great demand for it and he never forgot this lesson.

While people thought he was mad, Edison carried out experiment after experiment to make a simple, cheap and effective electric light bulb which would be better than gas lighting and suitable for use in the home. What he needed was an inexpensive filament which would neither overheat nor use too much current. He tried hundreds of metals and fibres until he found a Japanese bamboo which gave him one thousand hours of light before burning out. His electric light bulbs which were perfected by 1879 were used to light New York City three years later.

He was a highly practical man and on the occasion of his electric lighting system first being used in the theatre for a performance of 'Iolanthe', he had no hesitation, when the lights dimmed in the interval, in stripping off his dress clothes and running down to the cellar to put the matter right and rescue the performance.

He had the habit of coming into his laboratory first thing in the morning and tossing a piece of paper with a rough drawing on it to one of his assistants and saying, 'Make that!' Once, when his assistant asked what the new invention would do, he was told that it would talk back to him. Edison had found out that a fixed needle cutting grooves in a cylinder of tin foil could trap the sounds of the human voice and play them back. So in 1877 was invented what the English called the gramophone and the Americans the phonograph.

## Things to do

A.  Answer these questions:
  1  Who invented the telephone?
  2  Who introduced the 'Kodak' camera?
  3  Who built the first practical typewriter?
  4  Whose name is linked with sewing machines?
  5  Name two of Edison's inventions.
B.  Make a neat copy of the diagram.
C.  Write your own account of any three of the inventions.

# The Inventors (2)

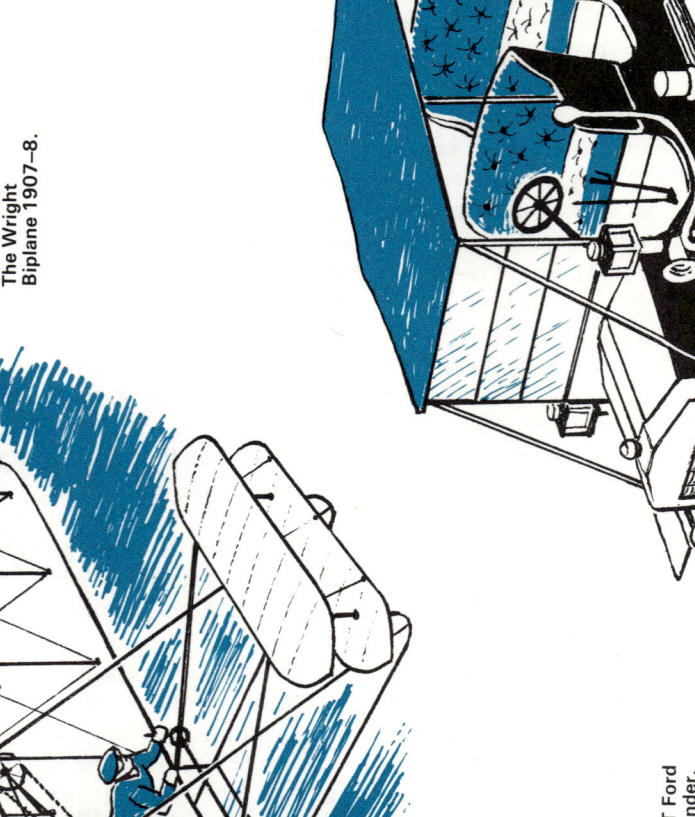

The Wright
Biplane 1907–8.

The Model T Ford
1909, 4-cylinder.
Top speed 40 m.p.h.
Low price—reliable motoring

# The Inventors (2)

Just as people laughed when Edison said he would invent a cheap light for every home, so no one believed Henry Ford (1863–1947) when he said that he would produce a light, reliable motor-car at a price that would suit the pockets of the mass of Americans.

Henry Ford was born in Michigan, the son of an Irish farmer who had emigrated to America in 1847. He started work as an engineering apprentice at sixteen and set up his own machine shop on his father's farm. He built a petrol engine to do heavy work on the farm and in 1893 perfected his first motor-car with a speed of twenty-five miles (40 km) per hour. By 1924 he was producing two million cars, trucks and tractors a year, and his Ford Motor Company was already world famous.

His secret was to standardise all parts and to put his cars together piece by piece, always in the same way, so that it became the automatic process of the assembly line. He took full advantage of mass production for the widest possible market. His most famous early model was the 'Model T Ford', which, the salesman would tell you, could be bought in any colour provided it was black!

Ford's technique of mass production on the assembly line was very widely copied in America and elsewhere. It tended to turn the workman into a robot and was heavily criticised in Charles Chaplin's film 'City Lights', but it certainly created motor-cars for the millions and when copied by other industries produced the astonishing variety of labour-saving gadgets demanded by Americans.

In 1893 two brothers, Wilbur and Orville Wright, opened a shop for the repair, sale and maintenance of cycles. Their real interest had always been flying and they had read every book on the subject they could get their hands on. They sent to the famous Smithsonian Institution for the latest information on the subject.

By 1899 they were ready to experiment themselves. They built a small kite-like glider to test their ideas about control in the air which they believed depended on twisting or warping the wings. They took their glider to Kitty Hawk, North Carolina, an area of high winds and flat sand dunes, and carried out tests. In 1900 they came back again with the first man-carrying glider, made more tests and then went home to try out over two hundred different types of wing in their home-made wind tunnel.

After their experiments with wings they added a tail with twin vertical planes to their glider because they now believed that the control of the machine in the air depended on the joint working of wings and tail. In 1902 they made glides of more than two hundred metres and were able to flatten out their angle of descent, which made landing smoother.

They added a petrol engine to their glider and in 1903 made four flights, the longest about three hundred metres. This was the first controlled flight by a man in a heavier-than-air machine. The brothers continued to experiment and increased the flights to twenty-four miles (40 km) and thirty minutes in 1905 and to two hours in 1908, the year when the U.S. War Department ordered its first aeroplane.

The Wright brothers worked out the science of flying by mathematics and by practical experiment. They paved the way for the Frenchman Blériot to fly the Channel in 1909, for the Englishmen Alcock and Brown to fly the Atlantic in 1919, and for the American Charles Lindbergh to fly solo from New York to Paris in 1927.

## Things to do

A. Answer these questions:
1 What did Ford decide to make?
2 What was his secret?
3 Name his most famous model.
4 Who pioneered flying in the U.S.A.?
5 Where did they make their tests?
6 When was the first powered flight made?

B. Make a neat copy of the diagram.

C. Tell the story in your own words of either Henry Ford or the Wright brothers.

# The Agricultural Revolution 1860–1900

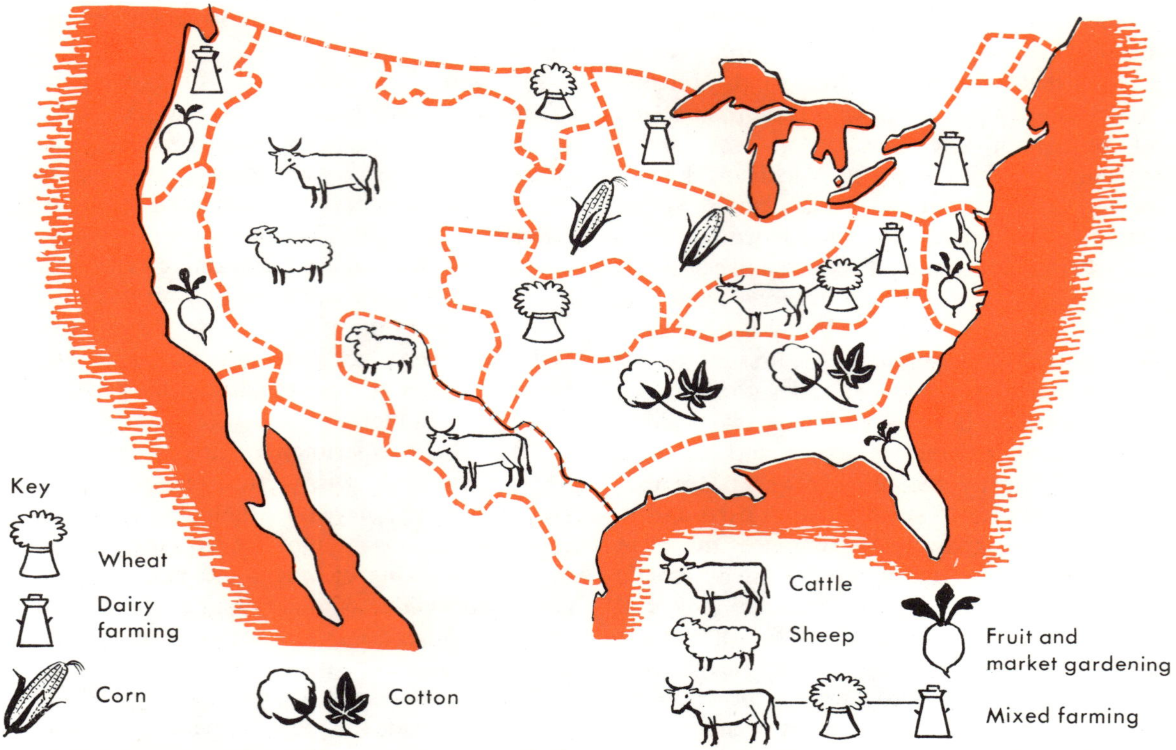

Key
Wheat
Dairy farming
Corn
Cotton
Cattle
Sheep
Fruit and market gardening
Mixed farming

LAND FOR FARMING
Homestead Act 1862

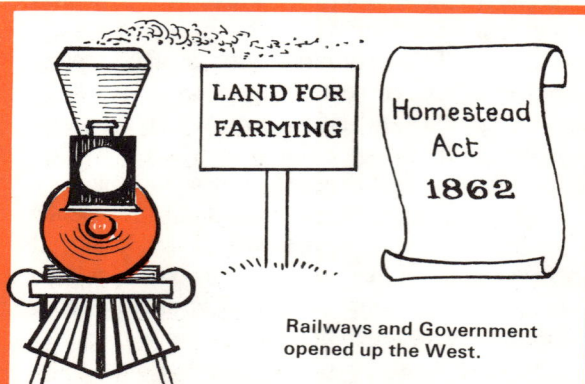

Railways and Government opened up the West.

COLLEGE OF AGRICULTURE

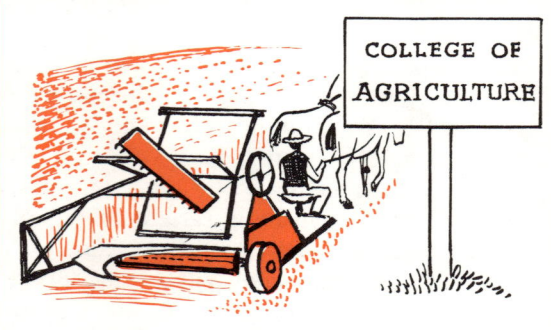

Farming became mechanised and scientific.

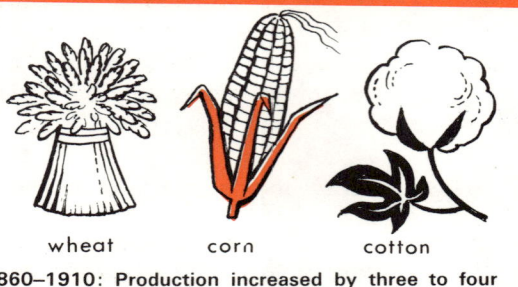

wheat
corn
cotton

1860–1910: Production increased by three to four times.

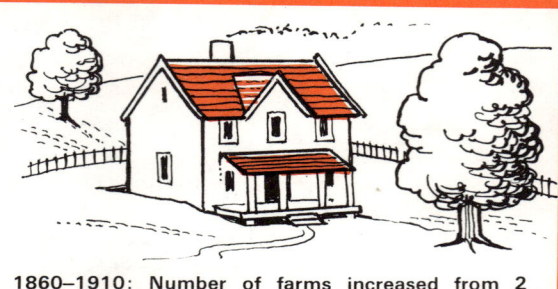

1860–1910: Number of farms increased from 2 millions to 6 millions.

# The Agricultural Revolution 1860–1900

The early American farmer was practically self-supporting. His bread, fruit, vegetables and milk came from the farm, his clothes from the sheep's back, his timber from the nearby forest and his harness and footwear from the local tannery. The farmer served the needs of his family and of the immediate locality.

From the time of the American Civil War to 1900, American farming changed very much. Firstly many more people decided to till the land. The high price of grain and meat both during and after the war encouraged more people to settle on the land. The railways opened up the West for the farmer. They carried him and his family, his tools and cattle to his new home and transported his meat and grain to new markets in the large cities on the east coast. The railway companies sold land cheaply on both sides of their track, in order to build up business for their lines.

Further encouragement to go west and farm came from the government. By the Homestead Act of 1862, American families were each offered one hundred and sixty acres (65 hectares) of land free of charge, if they would agree to live on their acres and cultivate them for at least five years. In 1889 thousands of settlers poured into Oklahoma to stake out farms and homes among the three thousand acres opened up to them by order of the government.

Shortage of labour and the growing size of the American farm made the farmer welcome the ever increasing variety of machinery which American industry pressed him to buy. By 1900, he could purchase a rotary plough which would turn over the soil, break it up, make drills in it and sow the grain all in one operation. When harvest-time came his combine harvester could reap, thresh, clean and bag the grain in one smooth process. Machinery brought the largest benefits, and the greatest economies, to the large farms of the West.

Farming became more scientific. The Federal government set up a Department of Agriculture which encouraged the building of Agricultural Colleges and the setting up of Research Stations in each state. People were trained in the latest farming techniques and measures were taken to fight animal diseases and plant pests. New plants and seeds were introduced into the U.S.A. Types of wheat especially resistant to disease were brought in from Canada and Russia. White Kaffir corn was imported from the oases of the Sahara and varieties of rice from the Far East were planted in Louisiana.

Once the better lands of the West were all occupied, settlers tried to farm the drier areas of the South-west. Here, government irrigation projects were helpful. The Theodore Roosevelt Dam on Salt River, Arizona, opened in 1907, provided water for two hundred thousand acres (80 000 hectares) of farm land. It was a forerunner of the famous Boulder Dam, opened on the Colorado River in 1935.

The changes in agriculture produced important results. Between 1860 and 1910 the number of farms in the U.S.A. increased from two millions to six millions and the acreage of land under agriculture doubled. The annual production of corn, wheat and cotton increased by three to four times. The American farmer fed a vast home population and produced a large surplus of food for sale overseas. He did this with a relatively smaller labour force.

It is doubtful whether the individual farmer was better off for much of the time. Prices of wheat, corn and cotton dropped markedly between 1860 and 1900 because of increased output, but railway charges which he had to pay and the interest on loans he borrowed to tide himself over difficult times, remained high. Linked to world markets and world prices for food, the farmer had to face the ups and downs of boom and depression and of war and peace.

## Things to do

A. Answer these questions:
   1. Whom did the early farmer serve?
   2. Give four reasons why farming changed after 1860.
   3. How did the government help farmers?
   4. Why did the farmer buy machinery?
   5. What did the federal government do?
   6. How did the changes affect farming?

B. Make a neat copy of the diagram.

C. Show how American farming changed between 1860 and 1900.

# The Revolution in Industry
# 1860–1900

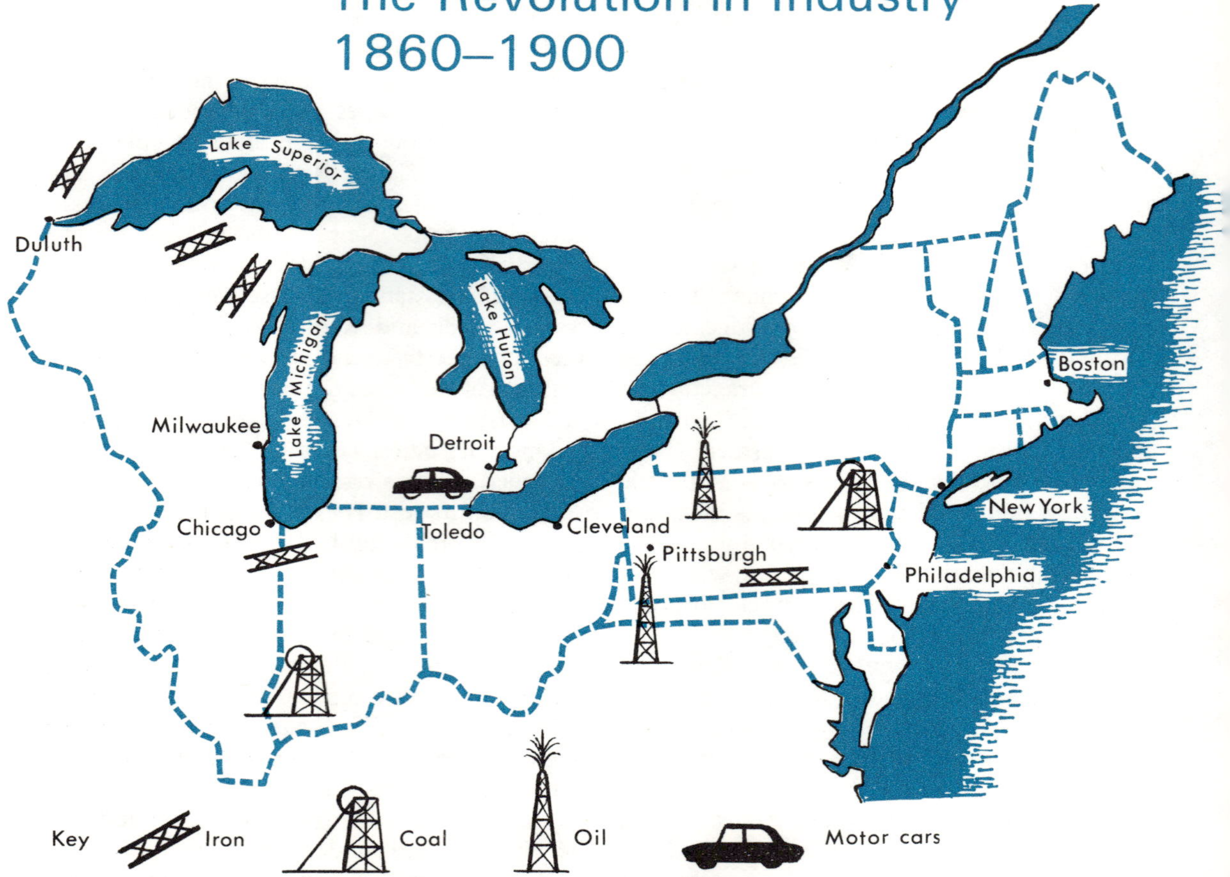

Lake Superior

Duluth

Lake Michigan

Lake Huron

Milwaukee

Detroit

Boston

Chicago

Toledo

Cleveland

Pittsburgh

New York

Philadelphia

Key    Iron    Coal    Oil    Motor cars

Large quantities of iron are discovered around Lake Michigan and Lake Superior.

New methods of making steel discovered by Bessemer (1856) and Siemens (1868).

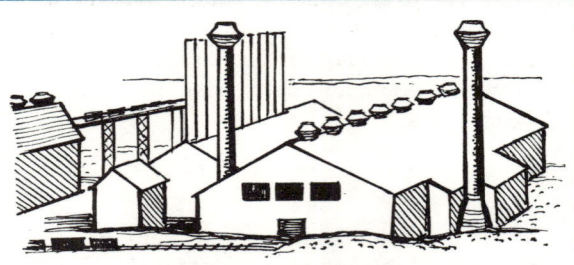

Andrew Carnegie (1835–1919) was the greatest steel manufacturer of the U.S.A.

The U.S.A. became an industrial country of big cities, high population and big business.

# The Revolution in Industry 1860–1900

In 1860 America was mainly an agricultural country and her industrial output was far below that of Britain. By 1900 America had become the leading manufacturing country in the world.

America's industrial growth was based on her iron and steel industries. Large quantities of iron ore were discovered around the shores of Lake Michigan and Lake Superior. The iron ore was carried to the growing centres of the iron industry at Chicago, Cleveland, Toledo, Milwaukee and Pittsburgh by rail or steamship. Further deposits of iron and coal were found in the South to make Birmingham, Alabama, another important industrial area.

The iron industry was given a vital boost in the second half of the nineteenth century by the discovery of new methods of making steel, which was the strongest and most useful metal that could be made from iron ore. In 1856 Henry Bessemer of Sheffield, England, found out how to make steel in large quantities and at reasonable cost. He heated iron and carbon in sealed vessels or 'converters' and burnt out the impurities in the molten metal, which had previously spoilt the steel, by passing a blast of air through the converter. In 1868 William Siemens of Swansea, Wales, made steel in an 'open hearth' furnace which allowed him to treat the molten liquid and remove any defects or impurities at any time in the process of manufacture. This was an even better way of making high-class steel. Both methods were adopted in America, which by 1900 had become the leading producer of steel in the world, with an annual output greater than that of Germany and Britain combined.

The most famous steel manufacturer in the U.S.A. was Andrew Carnegie (1835–1919) whose parents came to Pittsburgh from Scotland in 1848. As a young boy Andrew worked in a cotton mill, then progressed to messenger boy and telegrapher for the Western Union Telegraph Company and finally to clerk and superintendent for the Pennsylvania Railroad Company at Pittsburgh.

Carnegie was one of the first people to foresee the huge demand that would arise for steel to make rails, locomotives, ships, bridges, buildings and even knives and forks. At the age of thirty-five he decided to put all his energy and his savings into the iron industry. He chose good men to look after his mills, mines and coalfields. He adopted the new methods of manufacture of Bessemer and Siemens. He wrung cheap rates out of railways and shipping lines to carry his steel to worldwide markets.

Carnegie controlled the whole process of steel manufacture from the load of coal and iron ore down to the finished steel. Everything was done on the largest possible scale and this became the pattern of American industry and business. The large organisation brought savings and removed competitors. Carnegie's huge Steel Company was matched by John D. Rockefeller's giant Standard Oil Company and by Cornelius Vanderbilt's railroad empire, which controlled nearly five thousand miles of lines from New York to the Middle West.

America became by 1900 an industrial country of great cities, high population and big business. Many people enjoyed a higher standard of living, new ways of travel, improved forms of communication and a great variety of labour-saving devices in home and factory. Great poverty, however, existed alongside great wealth. America had city slums as well as millionaires. Periods of unemployment alternated with periods of boom and there were violent battles between workers and employers in the years of depression.

## Things to do

A. Answer these questions:
1 What helped the growth of industry?
2 Name two new methods of making steel.
3 Who was the greatest American steel manufacturer?
4 What was special about Andrew Carnegie?
5 How did the build-up of industry affect America?

B. Make a neat copy of the diagram.

C. Write about: Bessemer, Siemens, Andrew Carnegie.

D. Describe the growth of American industry 1860–1900.

# Steel (Carnegie) and Oil (Rockefeller)

**Andrew Carnegie, 1835–1919**

**John D. Rockefeller, 1839–1937**

# John D. Rockefeller and Oil

John D. Rockefeller was born on a small farm in the state of New York in 1839. His father who was something of a trickster and sold 'magic' medicines to unsuspecting country folk, was rarely at home and the boy was brought up by his deeply religious Scottish mother. When she whipped the boy for something he did not do and he complained, she told him not to fret, for the whipping would do for the next time.

He worked on the farm until he was sixteen, but at ten years of age he had saved enough money in a blue china bowl to lend a neighbouring farmer fifty dollars at seven per cent interest. He was most impressed a year later when his fifty dollar loan was paid back with three dollars and fifty cents interest. This was more than he had earned in ten days hoeing potatoes, and he 'decided to make money work for him'.

He left the farm in 1855 to take a post in Cleveland as an accounts clerk with a trading company which dealt in meat and grain. By six-thirty every morning he was at work, squinting down at the ledgers by the light of whale-oil lamps. At weekends he taught Sunday School classes at the Erie Street Baptist Church. His favourite text was, 'See thou a man diligent in his business? He shall stand before kings.'

In 1858 he started up his own meat and grain business in partnership with an Englishman called Clark. Their business prospered, especially during the Civil War when the price of grain and meat rose.

In 1859 oil was discovered in large quantities at Oil Creek, near Titusville, in Pennsylvania. The wagons which carried the crude oil to the refineries, where it was turned into kerosene (paraffin) for heating and lighting, passed by the door of Rockefeller's warehouse. In 1863 he put all his savings into the new oil-refining firm of Andrews, Clark and Rockefeller. Andrews was the technical man and handled the refining process, Clark dealt with the men at the oil-fields and Rockefeller took charge of the sale of refined oil and of general finance.

In 1865 Rockefeller bought the business from Clark and the new firm of Rockefeller and Andrews enjoyed the benefits of the growing demand for kerosene. From this original refining company grew the world famous Standard Oil Company, set up in 1870. Within ten years it was refining ninety-five per cent of all the oil produced in the U.S.A.

Rockefeller built up a vast world-wide organisation. He created great wealth and hundreds of thousands of jobs. He believed in a quality product, manufactured by the best plant and the best workmen at the cheapest cost and delivered to the customer in the most efficient manner. He paid his workmen at the highest rates. Americans were frightened by the immense power he built up and by the ruthless way he bought up his rivals or forced them out of business.

The real importance of Rockefeller's work was that he gave the American oil industry a strong and efficient organisation in its early stages. In the twentieth century with the invention of the petrol engine, oil was refined for its gasoline (petrol) rather than its kerosene (paraffin). It became one of the world's most important sources of power and America's most important industry. Vast oil-fields were opened up in the twentieth century in California, Oklahoma and Texas.

## Things to do

A. Answer these questions:
   1 Where and when was Rockefeller born?
   2 What was his first job? His second?
   3 When did he go into business? With whom?
   4 Why was 1863 important for him?
   5 What did he set up in 1870?
   6 Why was he feared?
   7 What did he achieve?

B. Make a neat copy of the diagram.

C. Tell the life story of John D. Rockefeller.

# To Help You Remember

1861 – 1865

Slavery and the Civil War

Vicksburg 1863

Gettysburg

Defeat for the South in the Civil War

C.P.U. – U.P. 1869

The Transcontinental Railroads

On the Chisholm Trail

SALOON HOTEL

Abilene—Cattle Town 1867–1871

Little Big Horn 1876

Wounded Knee 1891

The last years for the Indians

The 'Huddled Masses' 1860–1930

Bell    Edison    Singer

Wright Bros.

Henry Ford

The Inventors (2)

The Barons of Industry
Andrew Carnegie    John D. Rockefeller

# To Help You Remember

The American Civil War of 18.. to 18.. was fought over two points, n.... s...... and the U.... of the American states. The publication of "U.... T...'s C...." and the hanging of I.... B.... stirred up emotions to fever pitch. The bombardment of F... S.... marked the beginning of the war.

In the Civil War the country was divided between N...... or U.... forces and S...... or C......... forces. General L.. was the most successful general for the South, General G.... for the N...h. The disasters at V....... and G........ made final defeat inevitable for the S...h.

One of the earliest American railways was drawn by h....s. It was called the M........... G...... railway. By 1860 important railway lines ran from B..... to B......, from P........... to C......, from B....... to St. L....s.

The next development was to build railways to span the continent. In May, 18.. the two lines built by the C...... P...... and the U.... P...... met at P........ P.... in U..h. Other trans-continental railways were the N....... P...... and the S.... F.. Competition from the a......... and from the a....... caused a sharp decline in the railways in the t........ century.

After the end of the Civil War the cattle drives were resumed. Texas L....... were driven up one of the three main trails, the C......, the W..... and the G....... and L....., to the northern railway towns of A......, D.... C..., and E.......h.

The Indians were driven out of their homelands by m....s, h.....s and s......s. They lost their l... and their b.......s. They won a great victory on the Little B.. H... river in 18.. but suffered a final defeat at W..... K... in 1891.

Large numbers of immigrants poured into America during the period 18.. to 19... They included people from the U..... K......, from G....., A....., I...., R.... and P....d.

The last quarter of the nineteenth century and the early years of the twentieth were a golden age for the American inventor. Some famous names from this period are: B..., E...., S.... and E.....n. The W..... brothers will always be remembered for their pioneer work on the a......., as will H.... F... for the production of a light, reliable, cheap motor-car.

American f...... changed very much between 18.. and 19... R...... opened up the West and the g........ offered l... to the settler who would farm it. The American farmer used more m....... and American farming became more s.......c. The annual production of c...., w.... and c... increased markedly but p..... fell sharply.

In 1860 America was mainly an a.......... country. By 1900 it was the leading m........... country in the world. America's i......... growth was based on i... and s...l. The greatest American steel manufacturer was A..... C......e.

John D. Rockefeller set up the S....... O.. C..... in 18... He gave the American o.. i....... a strong and efficient organisation. In the twentieth century vast new oil fields were opened up in C........., O....... and T...s.

## Things to do

Write out the above passage in your note-book, filling in the blanks. You will find the answers on the opposite page or in the earlier chapters of the book.